CROWOOD SPORTS GUIDES
NETBALL
SKILLS • TECHNIQUES • TACTICS

Anita Navin

THE CROWOOD PRESS

First published in 2008 by
The Crowood Press Ltd
Ramsbury, Marlborough
Wiltshire SN8 2HR

www.crowood.com

British Library Cataloguing-in-Publication Data
A catalogue record for this book is available from the British Library.

ISBN 978 1 84797 042 8

Dedication
To Mum, Dad and Denise whose support and encouragement are priceless.

Acknowledgements
The author and publishers would like to thank the following for their help in the production of this book: Mark Pritchard (for the photographs, except where credited otherwise), Northumbria University (for the use of their sports facilities), Team Northumbria Netball Squad and all other Super League squad players (the players in the photographs).

Disclaimer
Please note that the author and the publisher of this book are not responsible or liable, in any manner whatsoever, for any damage, or injury of any kind, that may result from practising, or applying, the techniques and methods and/or following the instructions described in this publication. Since the exercises and other physical activities described in this book may be too strenuous in nature for some readers to engage in safely, it is essential that a doctor is consulted before undertaking such exercises and activities.

Illustrations by Keith Field.

Typeset and designed by D & N Publishing
Lambourn Woodlands, Hungerford, Berkshire.

Printed and bound in Singapore by Craft Print International.

CROWOOD SPORTS GUIDES
NETBALL
SKILLS • TECHNIQUES • TACTICS

CONTENTS

Diagram Key

Use the following key for the diagrams used throughout this book.

GK	Goal keeper
GD	Goal defence
WD	Wing defence
C	Centre
WA	Wing attack
GA	Goal attack
GS	Goal shooter

Player move

Ball path

GS   **GS**

Attacking player   **Defending player**

PART I

INTRODUCTION TO NETBALL

CHAPTER 1

THE GAME OF NETBALL

The History of Netball

Netball was originally called basketball, and was invented in the United States of America in 1891. The game was first introduced in England in 1895 when an American called Dr Toles visited Madame Bergman Osterberg's Physical Training College. The students who were taught the game continued to educate the students who entered the college each year. The game was constantly changing as no printed rules were available, and each year the students thought they could improve the rules and regulations.

At the college the game was played using two waste-paper baskets as the goals, hung on the walls at each end. The walls formed the boundaries, so the ball was never out of play. The college relocated to Dartford from Hampstead, and in 1898 an American lady visited the college and taught the game as it was being played by women in the USA. The

Netball in 1907.
(Reproduced by courtesy of England Netball)

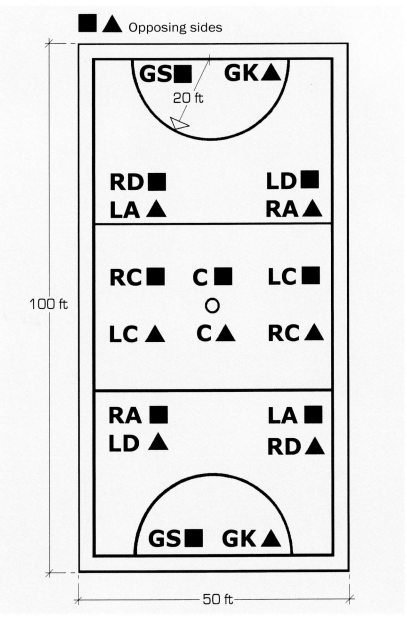

The court layout and positions in 1901.

ABOVE & *RIGHT: The first Netball World Championships, England versus Jamaica 1963. (Reproduced by courtesy of England Netball)*

England Commonwealth Games squad with bronze medals in 1998. (Reproduced by courtesy of England Netball)

baskets were replaced with rings, the court divided into three, the obstruction rule introduced, and a larger ball was used. Later, as the students became qualified teachers and began teaching in schools, there was a need for some uniform rules.

The Ling Association (now referred to as the Physical Education Association) was founded in 1899: its members were mainly from Madame Osterberg's college, and it seemed appropriate to allow this group to undertake the writing and publication of the rules. In 1901 the rules were first published: this edition contained 250, and they conveyed many differences and developments, including the introduction of a shooting circle, the throw-in, non-interference with any player or the ball, a ball of specific dimension, fixed posts, and rings with nets. As a result of the changes, the game was called 'net ball', which ultimately became 'netball'.

These are some of the key landmarks:

1905   English rules are introduced into the USA, Canada, France, South Africa as well as Wales, Scotland and Ireland.
Rules are sold in India, Canada, Burma, New Zealand, Australia, Jamaica, USA, Sweden, France and Denmark.

1926   Inaugural meeting in London of the All England Women's Netball Association. More than 250 delegates and schools, clubs and colleges were represented.

1932   First inter-county tournament held.

1947   Publication of the official netball magazine.

1949   First international at Wembley – Scotland v. Wales v. England.

1956   International match v. Australia at Harringay.

1957   Meeting of representatives from New Zealand, Great Britain, Australia, South Africa and the USA to discuss international rules; it was also agreed that a World Championship would be held every four years.

1963   First World Championship held in Eastbourne, England.

1988   U21 World Youth Championship held in Canberra as part of the Australian bicentenary celebrations, and its success led to the event being organized every four years.

1998   Netball included in the Commonwealth Games programme for the first time in Kuala Lumpur, where Australia took gold, New Zealand silver and England bronze.

Netball Super League teams in action.

Netball in England is now a leading sport for women, and with the introduction of the Netball Super League (NSL) in October 2005, the profile of the sport has grown dramatically. With television coverage the game is attracting thousands of viewers on a regular basis, and this top level competition for our élite players will undoubtedly contribute to England's ultimate target of being number one in the world.

The International Federation of Netball Associations (IFNA)

The International Federation of Netball Associations ('IFNA') is the sole governing body for netball throughout the world. Membership of IFNA is open to national netball associations, and currently IFNA has just over forty members grouped into five regions – Africa, Asia, the Americas, Europe and Oceania – each with their own regional federation. Regional federations are an integral part of IFNA, and assist in the implementation of IFNA policies in their respective regions.

IFNA is responsible for the rules of netball, a game played by upwards of twenty million people worldwide. Within the Commonwealth, netball has more active participants than any other sport. The IFNA vision, values and aims are outlined here:

Vision
- A vibrant and exciting global game.

Values
IFNA is committed to achieving high quality outcomes by:
- working together as a team;
- continually striving for excellence;
- drawing on best practices.

IFNA logo.
(Reproduced by courtesy of England Netball)

The aims of IFNA are:
- To encourage increased participation in netball.
- To continue to develop and foster interest in the sport at all levels and ages.
- To recognize and promote international competition.
- To encourage and develop high standards of administration, instruction and officiating in all regions.
- To establish, safeguard, enforce, review and amend, as necessary, the rules of netball.
- To encourage research and development and the dissemination of information in all areas relating to netball.
- To liaise with other governing bodies and international sporting federations.
- To strive for netball to become an Olympic programmed sport.

IFNA is managed by:
- Congress
- A board of directors
- Secretariat

In accordance with:
- Memorandum and articles
- Regulations
- Handbook
- Policies

IFNA also documents some clearly defined goals, which are:
- To build a global brand and profile for netball as an exciting and highly competitive sport.
- To establish strong and successful alliances and partnerships with international organizations, businesses and the media.
- To attract resources to benefit and support the global growth, development and profile of the game.
- To facilitate and promote a vibrant network to assist regions with the development of the game.
- To work with, and provide support to, regions to increase the membership of IFNA.
- To set the standards by which the game is led, managed and played.
- To facilitate and promote world class international competition.

More information can be found at: http://www.netball.org

The Accredited Netball Club

The Club Action Planning Scheme (CAPS) is an accreditation programme that allows clubs to seek a quality stamp, indicating that they provide certain standards, from England Netball. The levels of achievement are graded in terms of bronze, silver and gold status. Alongside this accreditation is the opportunity to apply and be assessed for the Sport England Clubmark, which evaluates the club based upon good practice for young people. Netball clubs can receive both awards, and by achieving the bronze status the Clubmark is also presented to the club.

CAPS accreditation confirms that the club has a clear structure, quality coaches and officials, volunteer opportunities, and a safe and equitable participation programme. The following areas are reviewed as part of the CAPS assessment:
- Duty of care and child protection
- Player, coach and official development
- Sports equity and ethics
- Club management
- Facilities and equipment
- Competition

As a result of the CAPS accreditation, local schools, local authorities, England Netball and Sport England will forge links and recommend the club to future participants.

England Netball Clubmark.
(Reproduced by courtesy of England Netball)

CHAPTER 2

GETTING STARTED: EQUIPMENT, PLAYING AND RULES

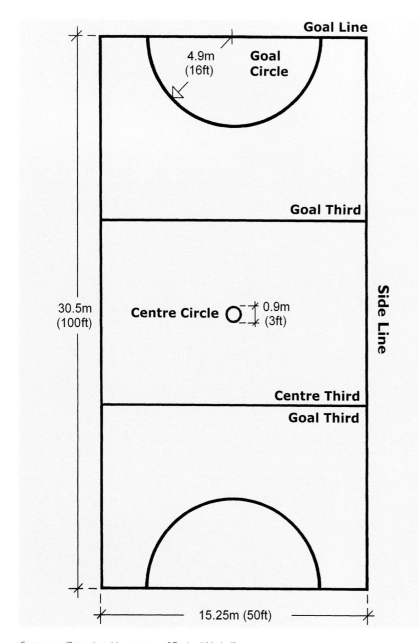

Court area. (Reproduced by courtesy of England Netball)

Netball is a game that is played both indoors and outdoors and on a firm surface; over the last decade it has gradually become more of an indoor game. However, several league matches and competitions are still held at outdoor venues on a concrete all-weather surface. It is recommended that indoors, the game is played on a court with a wooden sprung floor, and for international matches the surface should be a sprung wooden floor with a suitable run-off beyond the lines of the court.

Equipment

The overall size of the court is 30.5m long and 15.25m wide. The longer sides are called 'side lines' and the shorter sides are referred to as 'goal lines'. The court is divided into three equal sections by two transverse lines drawn parallel to the goal lines: these are called 'thirds of the court'. The three sections are referred to as the 'centre third' and the two 'goal thirds'. Within each goal third there is a semi-circle with a radius of 4.9m, its centre at the mid-point of the goal line. The semi-circle is referred to as the 'goal circle'. A circle of 0.9m marks the centre of the court, and this is termed the 'centre circle'.

The Goalposts

Two goalposts are placed one at either end of the court: they are vertical and stand 3.05m high. A metal ring is placed at the top of the post: it has an internal diameter of 380mm and projects horizontally 150mm from the top of the post, and this is fitted with a net so that it is clearly visible. Padding is placed around the post, and this should extend the full length of the post to provide protection for the players. Often goalposts are now sunk into the ground and therefore do not have a metal base; however, should a base be used, this must not project on to the court area. The goalpost is placed so that the back of the post is at the outside of the goal line. For international matches there would always be a post inserted into the ground.

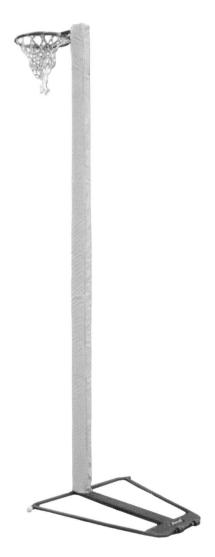

Goalpost.
(Reproduced by courtesy of England Netball)

The Ball

The ball must be a size 5 netball for the full game. If the modified game of high five is played, then a size 4 netball is used. The ball should weigh between 400 and 450g, and must be of leather, rubber or similar material.

England's Tamsin Greenway in modern kit.

The Playing Kit

It is essential that the correct footwear is worn by all players, and it is recommended that a specific netball shoe is purchased. The company Asics has designed a range of netball shoes to suit all playing standards, and the protection and support provided by these shoes have been developed as a result of research into the modern game. Playing kit is in the form of either a skirt and a shirt, or a dress. The training kit bag should contain a pair of shorts or skirt, a T-shirt, a towel and a water bottle.

The Players

A netball squad contains a maximum of twelve players, with only seven allowed to take the court at any time. No game can commence unless there are at least five players on the court, with one of those playing centre. Teams can make changes to the playing positions of the team, and/or make substitutions during an interval, or when play is stopped for injury or illness. There is no limit on the number of substitutions, provided they are taken from the twelve named for the match.

There are seven playing positions in the game of netball, and each player wears a bib, carried on the front and back of the playing kit and above waist height, with letters that represent the abbreviation for one of these positions; these letters must be 150mm high. The playing positions are as follows:

GK	Goal keeper	1	2		
GD	Goal defence	1	2	3	
WD	Wing defence		2	3	
C	Centre		2	3	4
WA	Wing attack			3	4
GA	Goal attack			3	4	5
GS	Goal shooter				4	5

Each player is restricted in terms of the court area they are allowed to play in; it is important to note that lines are considered to be a part of the area they surround.

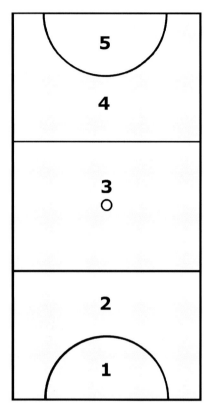

The playing positions – see list previous page. (Reproduced by courtesy of England Netball)

Rules

The rules presented here are correct at the time of going to print. The International Federation of Netball Associations (IFNA) reviews the rules on a four-yearly cycle following a World Championship; those presented here are current until 2011.

Duration of the Game

Netball is generally played over four quarters, each of 15min duration; the interval between the first and second, and third and fourth quarters is 3min, with a 5 or 10min interval at half-time. The duration of the interval is to be decided by the organiser prior to the start of the competition. The teams change ends at the end of each quarter. Where teams play more than one game in a day, the duration of these games is at the discretion of the officials, and should take into account the developmental level of the participants.

Officials

Two umpires must be in attendance to officiate at a game of netball, and there could also be scorers and timekeepers allocated at some competitions and matches. The team officials consist of a coach, a manager, a captain, and up to three other personnel, at least one of whom must be a primary care person. The primary care person must be qualified to diagnose and treat injury or illness, for example a doctor or physiotherapist. The full complement of officials would be present at any international match or competition.

The umpire must ensure that all players are safe in terms of playing kit, jewellery, adornments, and the correct length of fingernails. The umpire must use a whistle to start and stop the game, to signal when a penalty is to be awarded for an infringement, to indicate that a goal has been scored, and to signal to the timekeepers to hold time for stoppages.

Team Officials

Coaching is allowed from the team bench whilst play is in progress and also during the intervals between quarters. Coaching is not allowed during a stoppage (when a time out, which has been called by a player from either team).

Stoppages

During a stoppage no coaching can take place but the team manager may approach the players at the sideline for the purpose of providing rehydration. The first stoppage for each team in each quarter or half shall be up to 2min and in that time the player and Primary Care person must decide if the player can continue. It is the responsibility of the Primary Care person to determine whether the player can continue and no other team official from the bench is permitted on the court.

For each subsequent stoppage for each team, the injured or ill player must leave the court and has thirty seconds to do so. The injury or illness must be treated courtside and not on the court. The injured player may subsequently be substituted or the position may be left vacant.

After a stoppage for injury or illness, when no substitution is made for a player unable to resume play, the injured or ill player or a substitute may not enter the game whilst play is in progress.

There is a blood policy and should a player be bleeding then the umpire shall decide the length of the stoppage and shall ensure play is restarted as soon as possible. Once again, only the Primary Care person can enter the court area.

Positioning of the Players for the Start of Play

The game begins with the centre in possession of the ball standing wholly within the centre circle (this can be on one or both feet); the opposing centre must be in the centre third, but is free to move. All other players must be in the goal third that is part of their playing area, and they are free to move. When the whistle is blown to start the game, any of these players can move into the centre third. After a goal the game is restarted with a centre pass, and these are taken alternately throughout the game. If at a Centre Pass the ball is still in the hands of the Centre when the whistle is blown to signal the end of a quarter or half and provided no other infringement by that team has been penalised, that team will take the pass after the interval.

The centre pass must be caught or touched by a player who is standing wholly within the centre third, or who lands with the first foot, or both feet, within the centre third.

A player preparing for the centre pass.

A player leaning on the ball to regain balance.

Offside

A player is offside if they enter an area other than the area designated for their allocated playing position. However, a player may reach over and take the ball from an offside area, or may lean on the ball in an offside area providing no physical contact is made with the ground in the offside area. Should the player make contact with the ground then a free pass is awarded where the infringement occurred, to the opposing team.

Out of Court

The ball is deemed out of court when:
a) it touches the ground outside the court;
b) it touches an object or person in contact with the ground outside the court, or is held by a player in contact with the ground, an object or a person outside the court.

If a ball rebounds off a part of the goalpost it is not out of court.

A player who has left the court area to retrieve a ball must be permitted direct re-entry to the court; however, if a player moves out of court for no valid reason – not to retrieve a ball, take a throw-in, or seek a better playing position on court – they may not enter the game whilst play is in progress. The player may take the court after a goal, after a stoppage, or following an interval.

Playing the Ball

After receiving the ball a player is allowed only 3sec with the ball before it must be released. A player can catch the ball with one or two hands, gain or regain control if it rebounds off the goalpost, bat or bounce the ball to another player without having had possession, and tip the ball in an uncontrolled manner once, or more than once, to catch it or direct it to another player. Whilst a player is able to roll the ball to herself, the ball cannot be rolled to another player. A player who falls when holding the ball must regain footing and throw the ball within 3sec.

Players are not allowed to use a fist, fall on the ball to gain possession, gain possession whilst lying, kneeling or sitting on the ground, or use the goalpost as a means of regaining balance for helping to direct the ball. A player who has caught or held the ball cannot throw the ball to herself, drop the ball and replay it, or replay the ball after a shot at goal, unless it touched a part of the goalpost.

There must always be space for a third person to move between the hands of the thrower and those of the receiver. The ball cannot be thrown over a complete third without being touched or caught by a player who has landed in that third, or is standing wholly within that third.

If two opposing players gain possession of the ball in quick succession, the umpire shall call 'Possession' and indicate the player who first caught the ball. Play shall continue with this player in possession of the ball.

Footwork

A player may receive the ball with one or both feet on the ground, or jump to catch it and land on one foot. The player is allowed to step with the other foot in any direction, pivoting on the landing foot. The landing foot may be lifted off the ground, but the ball must be thrown, or a shot taken at goal, before this foot is regrounded. A player may receive the ball whilst both feet are grounded, or land on both feet simultaneously and then step with either foot. The foot that is not

moved is considered to be the landing foot, and this may be lifted but not regrounded until after the ball has been released. Nor is the player permitted to drag or slide the landing foot.

Scoring a Goal

A goal is scored when the ball is thrown or batted over and completely through the ring by the goal shooter or goal attack from any point within the goal circle. If the defending player within the circle deflects a shot for goal and the ball passes completely through the ring, a goal is scored. The shooter may not have contact with the ground outside the shooting circle either during the catching of the ball or whilst holding it, and must obey the footwork and 3sec possession rule.

Obstruction

A player may attempt to intercept or defend the ball from a distance on the ground of 0.9m from the player in possession. This distance is measured from the landing foot which is on the ground, or if the landing foot has been lifted, the distance is measured from the spot on the ground from which the foot was lifted. Obstruction occurs if the defender lessens the distance, or if they jump and land within 0.9m and interfere with the throwing or shooting action of the player in possession. Within this distance a player is not obstructing if the arms are outstretched to catch or intercept a pass or feint pass, to gain a rebound from a shot at goal, or if they momentarily stretch out their arm to signal for a pass.

A goal being scored.

A player marking the ball.

A player may defend an opponent who has elected to go out of court provided that the defender remains within the court area; but a player who is standing out of court is unable to defend a player who is on the court.

Contact

No player may contact an opponent accidentally or deliberately in a manner that interferes with the play of that opponent. When in the act of defending, a player may not move into the path of an opposing player who is committed to landing in a particular area, or position so closely that the player cannot move without contacting, or place a hand on the ball or knock it out of the ball carrier's possession.

Awarding Penalties

All penalties except the toss-up are awarded to the team, which means that any player allowed in the area of the infringement can take the penalty. The penalties outlined below are awarded in the game of netball unless the umpire decides to play the advantage rule.

When taking a penalty the player must take up the position clearly directed and indicated by the umpire before playing the ball and throw the ball within three seconds. The player must also obey the footwork rule and the first foot placed at the point indicated is equivalent to the landing foot in a one foot landing or to receiving the ball with one foot grounded.

The player taking the penalty must be allowed in the area where the infringer was standing unless this places the non-offending team at a disadvantage. Both the player taking the penalty and the offending player/s must take up the positions as indicated by the umpire before the ball can be played.

Discipline

Players and team officials will be penalized for any infringements caused between the

AWARDING PENALTIES	
Name	Infringement
Free pass	Footwork, offside, lost possession, throwing over a third
Penalty pass or penalty pass or shot	Obstruction, contact, when a defender causes the goalpost to move, which interferes with a shot
Throw-in	The ball goes out of court – given to the opposing team in relation to the last player on the court who had contact, or the player who had contact with the ball but had made contact with the ground, a person or object out of the court
Toss-up	Simultaneous event between opposing players; gain simultaneous possession, go offside, contact, out of court or both knock the ball out of court

scoring of a goal and the restart of play, between the ball going out of court and the throw-in, and between the award and taking of any penalty on court. The umpire will penalize the team by awarding the appropriate penalty as soon as play restarts.

A player or team official must not deliberately delay play, persistently break the rules, or play in a dangerous manner, and should this occur – or indeed, any apparent misconduct – the umpire will penalize the offending player/team official. This may also include persistent infringing of one rule or several rules in combination. Players can be suspended from a game for a given period of time, and unless extreme, the player will have received a warning prior to this suspension.

A team must take the court when requested to do so by the umpire. The umpire shall notify the teams when there are thirty seconds and ten seconds remaining prior to the start of a game and the end of an interval. At the ten-second notification the players must move to their playing positions for the start or restart of play. If a team fails to take the court by the start or restart of play the umpire shall penalize for deliberate delaying of play and if the team fail to take the court within one minute of the start or restart the umpire shall award the game to the non-offending team.

A toss-up being taken.

CHAPTER 3

HIGH FIVE NETBALL

Aims and Objectives

High five is a modified version of the full game of netball, and England Netball advocates its inclusion in any school and/or club for boys and girls aged nine to eleven. The initial experience of any game is the most definitive in determining a new player's future participation, and high five will promote enjoyment, and enable young people to play a game that equates to their level of development; it also ensures a progressive introduction to the full seven-a-side game.

The rules are modified to allow players freedom around the court; such modifications also give the younger players a bit more time to process information and then act on it. The game encapsulates the notion of teamwork, and introduces young people to the roles of scorer and timekeeper.

Rules and Procedures

High five is played on a full-size netball court, though in some instances the court can be smaller; however, the shooting circles should always remain the same size. The goalpost is lowered for this game, and should stand at 2.74m; a size 4 ball is used.

The squad should consist of a minimum of seven and a maximum of nine players, with only five on the court at any one time. A match should be played over four quarters, each lasting 6min with a 2min interval between each quarter. However, some festivals are held with several teams, and games can be 5min each way. At a festival the same rotations are applied, and it will take two games to complete the rotation as opposed to one. The high five positions and associated playing areas are shown in the illustration.

During the interval the squad should rotate positions: this should ensure that no player is off the court consecutively, and

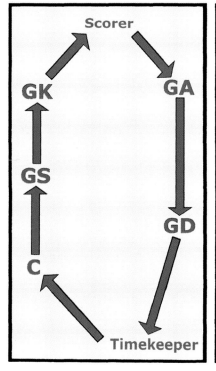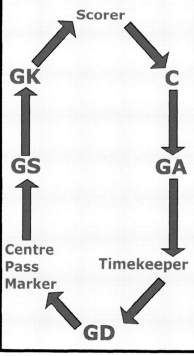

The possible rotation patterns for a high five squad of seven, eight and nine. (Reproduced by courtesy of England Netball)

that all players have taken at least one off-court role (timekeeper, centre-pass marker or scorer). Substitutions are permitted at any time in the event of injury or illness. The rotation systems allow young players the chance to experience all positions in netball, which supports the notion of a non-specialized approach to playing the game in a player's early years. Whilst the seven-a-side rules are applied in most instances, there are certain modifications. Thus a player:

- must not defend the ball carrier from less than 1m;
- can hold the ball for 4sec;
- is not permitted to mark the ball carrier with outstretched arms;
- in possession must be permitted an unimpeded throwing or shooting action;
- defending is allowed one jump to intercept a throw or shot from at least 1m away.

Coaching a Session of High Five Netball

Children must be provided with a fun and enjoyable session that is progressive and provides realistic challenges. There is a need to ensure that all sessions facilitate the learning and development of skills, and where possible a coach should try and encourage teamwork and social interaction.

Players learn from doing, so it is vital that demonstrations are used and that talk time by the coach is kept to a minimum. A demonstration should be shown two to three times, and the coach should check that the players understand what is required before they go to their areas to work. A question such as 'What will you do now?' is better than 'Do you understand?', because the latter often prompts a 'yes' response, but the coach may then find the group does not understand, whereas the first question demands an understanding of the task in that the subsequent action must be correct.

As a coach you must move around the whole group, ensuring that all players have been observed. In terms of good practice there should be adequate work-to-rest periods, with time given to players for drinking some water. Session duration should be between 45min and 1hr for this age group.

The following activities could be included within a coaching session: warm-up activities, skill practices and game activities.

The high five court, playing positions and playing areas. (Reproduced by courtesy of England Netball)

Warm-up Activities

Catchers in the Third: There are three catchers, and they must each wear a bib. Players must stay within the third area, and the objective of the game is for the catchers to tag as many players as they can in a one-minute period. When a player is tagged they collect a cone and stay in the game. At the end of the minute the players' cones are counted to give the catchers a total score. The last three players 'in' take over as the new catchers, and the game can be repeated. For more able players the area for the game can be reduced each time the catchers are replaced – for example, half the third area, or ultimately into the shooting circle. (Up to twelve players per third area is recommended.)

Dishes and Domes: The game is played between two teams within a third area. Approximately sixteen cones are placed randomly throughout the area, some turned up like a dish, the others in their normal position like a dome. Each team is allocated 'dishes' or 'domes', and they must move around the area placing as many of the cones as possible in their given shape. Both teams will be competing within the area to ensure they have the highest number of 'domes' or 'dishes' after a one-minute period. They should have no contact with each other, and the cones must not be moved from their original position. (Four to six players per team are recommended.)

Skill Practices

Vision: This is played in fours with a ball. The ball is always passed to A, and A must pass the ball to a player other than the one she received from. Another ball can be added, which will put the worker A under more pressure to find a free player to pass to. The practice starts static, and can be progressed so that the receivers are all moving when A is looking to pass.

Interception: In groups of six with a ball. Four players form a square, and the defender is positioned in the centre. Two balls are passed between two players on each side of the square. An individual holds up cue cards outside the grid, and the defender must time the run for the interception, calling out the colour of the card as she moves to take the ball. This can be progressed so that two defenders work in the square and begin to communicate with each other, each taking any intercept on their own side.

Game Activity

Two versus Two to Goal: Using half of the court, six players take up position on each sideline. The ball is placed on a cone in the centre of the court. Each player is given a number from one to six, and two numbers are called out. When two numbers are called, the players move to try and be the first to pick up the ball: whichever team gets the ball becomes the attacker. With the other pair defending, they must try to work the ball to goal, abiding by high five rules, and try and score a goal once in the shooting circle. If the ball is intercepted, the defence must make three passes before they can have an attempt at goal. When the ball is out of play at the backline, or if a goal has been scored, the ball must be returned to the start and two more numbers called for the game to restart.

Umpiring High Five Netball

As an umpire it is vital that you have a good understanding of the rules, and you must be confident when taking on this role. An umpire must give their decision clearly and simply to assist the players in their interpretation. Where possible the umpire must assist those that lack knowledge and skill, and should always encourage all players.

Every umpire should be equipped with a copy of the rules for reference, a whistle looped on a cord around the neck, a stopwatch, two pencils, and a scorecard for scorers to use.

When calling an infringement the umpire must follow this five-step guide:
1 Blow the whistle.
2 Call the infringement (e.g. offside blue centre).
3 State the penalty (e.g. free pass).
4 Say whose ball it is (e.g. to the red team).
5 Indicate where the pass is to be taken. The umpire must move with the game in order to have a good view of play, however this must not involve moving on to the court, with the exception of taking a toss-up.

CHAPTER 4

EFFECTIVE COACHING IN NETBALL

The International Federation of Netball Associations (IFNA) recognizes that there are over sixty countries involved in the sport, spanning five regions of the world including the Americas, Asia, Africa, Oceania and Europe. Coaching is at the heart of all development programmes, and is deemed to be the most critical factor in the development of a player. Playing nations all advocate a player-centred approach to coaching, and stress the need for a coach to be knowledgeable in the science and art of coaching. To be successful a coach must have the knowledge of technical and tactical components of performance, along with the necessary communication and inter-personal skills. Many of the principles advocated in the new United Kingdom Coaching Certificate are supported and promoted in all playing nations across the globe.

UKCC LEVELS

Level	What the qualified coach will be able to do
Level 5	Generate, direct and manage the implementation of cutting-edge coaching solutions and programmes.
Level 4	Design, implement and evaluate the process and outcome of long-term/specialist coaching programmes.
Level 3	Plan, implement, analyse and revise annual coaching programmes.
Level 2	Prepare for, deliver and review coaching session(s).
Level 1	Assist more qualified coaches, delivering aspects of coaching sessions, normally under direct supervision.

The United Kingdom Coach Qualification Framework (UKCC)

The Netball UKCC is about supporting our great game, and making coaching better and therefore supporting our players of today and tomorrow. Netball Scotland, Welsh Netball and England Netball are all working together to develop an education programme to develop our coaches in all three countries.

The United Kingdom Coaching Certificate (UKCC) is a government-led strand of work that arose from the recommendations of the coaching task force that reported in September 2002. Thirty-one sports are involved in this UK-wide initiative, and are recognized in three phases. Netball is a phase two sport and has received funding from Sport England to develop the UKCC for netball.

The UK Coaching Certificate is an endorsement of sports-specific coach education. It ensures that sports are delivering the best available, athlete-centred coaching both in recreational, development and performance environments. It is a joint netball development between England Netball, Welsh Netball and Netball Scotland. The UKCC will significantly change the shape and quality of coach education within and across netball. In the future England Netball will be a formalized education provider of vocational qualifications that are appropriately developed, delivered, resourced, assessed and awarded.

How will the UKCC benefit coaches? The UKCC is a five-level coaching structure (see above).

KEY POINT

Overall the UKCC will:
- Enhance coaching skills, linked to the player pathway.
- Raise the profile of, and professionalize sports coaching.
- Offer more flexible coach-centred training programmes.
- Give UK-wide recognized qualifications.
- Provide a benchmark for employers and deployers of coaches.
- Ensure that core coaching skills are recognized and transferable between sports.
- Ensure a UK-wide endorsement of top quality, safe coaching.

The England Netball Code of Conduct for Coaches

In order to promote high standards in coaching, England Netball has outlined their code of conduct for all coaches, as set out below. A coach should observe the following guidelines:

1 Know and adhere to the England Netball duty-of-care guidelines.
2 Be responsible for setting and monitoring the boundaries between the player and the coach.
3 Be concerned primarily with the well-being, safety and protection of the player.
4 Take all reasonable steps to establish a safe working environment.
5 Be punctual at all training sessions, matches and meetings.
6 Be responsible for planning, co-ordinating, delivering and evaluating the sessions.
7 Ensure that all they do is in keeping with the regular and approved practice of England Netball.
8 Be responsible for communicating and co-operating with registered medical and ancillary practitioners in the diagnosis, treatment and management of a performer's medical and psychological problems. Where there is no medical intervention, be able to make responsible judgements on not playing an injured player.
9 Hold current affiliation to England Netball, and be responsible for arranging adequate insurance to cover all aspects of their coaching practice.
10 Attend appropriate England Netball coaching courses, and hold at least the Level 1 coach award before coaching alone.
11 Be responsible for regularly seeking ways of increasing their personal and professional development.
12 Be responsible for ensuring that the player's training is of the appropriate frequency and level for their age, maturity and ability.
13 Be responsible for discouraging players from violating the rules.
14 Educate players in the danger of taking banned substances that enhance their performance, and reinforce the rules relating to such offences.
15 Accept responsibility for a player's behaviour when in a sporting environment.
16 Reach individual agreements with the players on what information collated by the coach is deemed to be confidential. However, the disclosure of information to a certain party will be necessary in the following circumstances:
  • when it is so judged for legal and medical reasons;
  • to protect children from abuse;
  • when health and safety is at risk;
  • in the event of disciplinary action of the player within netball.
17 Display high personal standards in their code of dress, health and cleanliness.
18 Never smoke whilst involved in coaching, selection and matches.
19 Refrain from drinking alcohol so soon before coaching that it affects their coaching performance in any way.
20 Be equitable and fair to all players.

Coaches working with young people must:
21 Attend an England Netball duty-of-care workshop.

Supporting the Athlete-Centred Approach

Adopting an athlete- or person-centred approach involves coaching the individual, not the skill, always ensuring that their needs and interests are met. This approach seeks to help individuals improve their own capabilities so they can achieve personal goals, and educates them to take charge of learning and solving problems for themselves. This athlete-centred approach identifies the sporting experience as being only one part of the athlete's life, and from the outset puts it in context with other important human experiences – for example education, career, family and health. The coach therefore assumes a holistic view of the individual, and this requires a facilitative inter-personal relationship between athlete and coach.

A successful coach will make the transition through three stages in terms of their behaviour in order to instil self-

A coach discussing issues with an athlete.

confidence in the individual and promote self-responsibility. In stage one the coach will coach skills, ensure safety and communicate procedural information, and ultimately the environment is coach-dependent. In stage two the coach begins to offer collaborative opportunities for the individual, which build upon self-management and self-determination skills; at this stage there is a gradual transition from coach-dependence to a shared decision-making context. In stage three there is greater athlete-dependence and personal autonomy in the learning process. This coaching approach accepts that experience is defined individually, and to succeed the coach must create a 'mastery' (or task-oriented) climate for learning.

Questioning is an important tool for a coach when promoting personal autonomy, and stimulates athletes to think

Performers receiving one-to-one feedback. Feedback is effective when given to a player on an individual basis and free from distractions.

A young performer leading a group in a practice.

for themselves. Gradually the coach should move from asking low-order questions that are often factual demanding only one answer (for example: Where should you focus when taking a shot at goal?), to higher order questions that require synthesis and the application of knowledge (for example: Why would the zone be effective against the opposition?).

A 'mastery' climate is best described by the work of Epstein (1989), who uses the acronym TARGET to outline six important structural features for coaches to consider for an effectual motivational climate. It is the perception of these structural features that constitutes the motivational climate. The features are as follows:

T *Tasks* should be designed that promote diversity, are novel and varied. The tasks should involve personal goal-setting, and be challenging. Feedback should be given from multiple sources, and peer reviews of performance should be part of the tasks. Standards for measuring progress should be self-referenced.

A *Autonomy* should be promoted through individuals taking control in the learning environment. Choices should be given within the sessions, and leadership roles should play a part in some tasks. The individual should take some responsibility for performance profiling, and the overall monitoring of performance.

R *Rewards* and *recognition* should avoid comparative performance outcomes such as winning or rankings. Praise and reward should be based upon individual performance improvements and effort.

G *Grouping* should be varied, and sessions should contain multiple grouping arrangements. The coach must foster an environment where individual differences are tolerated.

E *Evaluation* should be based upon self-referenced criteria and mastery. Evaluation should be private and meaningful, with the individual contributing fully to the evaluation process.

T *Timing* of events in a session should be considered in relation to the ability, volume and intensity with which an individual can perform in practice, to their attentional capabilities, and their rates of learning.

In contrast, the coach who promotes a performance- (or ego-) oriented climate and takes full control in the sessions, will demotivate individuals. Here the coach promotes peer comparisons and doing better than others as being the only way to measure success. The individuals who continue to be coached in this context rely heavily upon the coach for decisions and strategy, and they are often unable to respond on court to the demands being placed upon them by the opposition.

Long-Term Athlete Development Model: Netball

The model outlined for netball is based upon the work of Dr Istvan Balyi, one of the world's leading experts in the field of long-term training and performance planning. Long-term athlete development (known as LTAD) is not an élitist model, but a pathway that provides the base for participating in life-long physical activity, as well as providing a sound framework for individuals who show the potential to compete at performance level.

Stage One – FUNdamentals

This is a crucial stage for developing movement vocabulary for physical activity (girls of five to eight, and boys of six to nine years of age). It is during this stage that individuals should develop their movement literacy and fundamental movement skills, which will underpin all sports and physical activities. This stage should be structured and fun, and the focus is on generic movement skill activities. Participation in a variety of sports should be encouraged, and speed should be developed using a range of game activities. Ability, balance and co-ordination – known as the ABCs – form a vital part of all planned activities and outcomes in this stage.

Stage Two – Learning to Train

In this stage (approximately age thirteen to sixteen), individuals should be learning to train with a limited emphasis on competition outcome and match play. There may be some competition in order to apply the technical skills to tactics, but this is in a ratio of 3:1 (training to competition). The skills of netball are introduced and developed with a range of practice design, including decision-making activities. Individuals are introduced to all netball positions and will be educated in the fundamentals of tactical work. There should still be an opportunity to participate in complementary sports (with similar energy requirements).

The coach must strive for quality movement, and should continue to refine such skills. The ancillary capacities are also developed in this learning phase, including education on warming up, cooling down, stretching, hydration and nutrition, recovery, relaxation, and focusing of attention. Individuals are introduced to the development of core strength activities, and flexibility exercises are an inherent part of the training programme. Medicine ball, Swiss ball and 'own bodyweight' exercises are evident within this stage.

If a young performer misses this stage it is unlikely that they will reach their full potential, and it is often the overload of competition in this phase that has a dramatic effect on athlete plateaus in the latter stages.

Stage Three – Training to Train

During this stage (approximately age fifteen to nineteen) the main priority is, according to Istvan Balyi, the time 'to build the engine', with an emphasis on aerobic conditioning. The fundamental technical skills are now progressed into more specific positional skills for the individual. Tactically an individual begins to learn the craft of a reduced number of positions or of a unit (for example, circle defence), and the tactical work is progressed.

This stage works on general physical conditioning, but there is now greater individualization of physical and technical training. The development of strength is a feature of this stage, and this involves developing a sound understanding of correct weight-lifting techniques. The time commitment to training now increases (high volume and a lower intensity), and there are competitions with specific performance outcomes developing tactical and psychological skills. The training to competition ratio remains at 3:1.

Stage Four – Training to Compete

The focus is now on 'optimizing the engine' (approximately age fifteen and over), and individuals are involved in higher volume training but with an increasing intensity. Greater emphasis is placed on the execution of skills and tactics in competitive situations. Training relates to position and the individual with an emphasis on advanced tactical preparation. The training to competition ratio is now 1:1 to enable the goals of this stage to be addressed and achieved.

Stage Five – Training to Win

This stage (age sixteen years and over) concerns peak performance, and is the final stage of the preparation. All of the physical, technical, tactical, psychological and ancillary capacities should now be developed so that the primary focus moves to the optimization of performance. Athletes will train to peak for certain competitions and major events such as the World Championships and Commonwealth Games. This stage concentrates on maintenance and fine tuning, and training is individualized throughout. The ratio of training to competition in this stage is 1:3.

Key Issues for the Coach

Young players are not miniature adults, and maturity may occur at different times and rates. The LTAD principles state that it would take an individual 10,000 hours of deliberate and structured practice to achieve their potential. In order to adopt an athlete- or person-centred approach the coach must consider the following three ages:

Chronological: Actual age from birth.
Developmental: Physical, social, emotional, cognitive development in comparison to individuals of the same age.
Training: The number of years the individual has been specializing and training in netball.

By considering all ages the coach will reduce the likelihood of injury, ensure that individuals have a better chance of reaching their potential, and ultimately will promote enjoyment and adherence to the netball programme. Individuals can be up to four years apart in terms of their maturity levels, and so the development age is a key consideration when planning training and performance programmes. Netball is a late specialization sport and so specialization is not advocated before the age of ten.

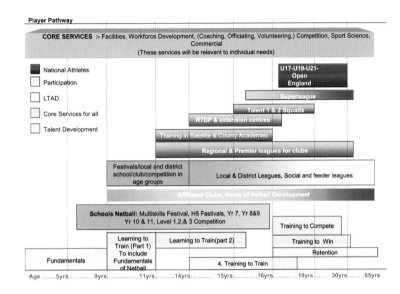

The netball player pathway. (Reproduced by courtesy of England Netball)

LTAD outlines key stages that are critical for the development of a young performer, and these are called 'windows of trainability'. For example, in terms of speed training a female will have the first window when she is between six and eight years of age, and a second window between eleven and thirteen years of age (chronological age).

The 'fundamentals' stage is a key stage that should be fun and enjoyable, allowing young participants the chance to acquire the movement skills required for success in any physical activity. The emphasis at this stage is on developing agility, balance, co-ordination and speed.

A coach working at this stage should plan and deliver sessions that incorporate a variety of movement skills and equipment, and offer short bursts of activities. Skill development practices should involve balancing using one or both feet, jumping in a variety of ways, and throwing and catching a range of implements, and the practices must stress spatial awareness when working in a space with others. This stage is not netball specific, and it is vital that all young people are coached in this phase to promote lifelong involvement in physical activity at whatever level, be it recreational or élite.

The netball talent development pathway begins at the 'learning to train' stage, providing the initial introduction to sport-specific training. At this stage individuals who demonstrate the potential to succeed in netball are offered places in regional and national talent programmes in order to develop their levels of performance. The player pathway, type of training and competition for each tier are illustrated in the table above.

THE WINDOWS OF TRAINABILITY FOR FEMALES

Stages	Skill	Speed	Strength	Aerobic
FUNdaMENTAL	Skill window 1	Speed window 1		
LEARNING TO TRAIN/practice				
TRAINING TO TRAIN		Speed window 2	Strength window 1	
				Aerobic window
TRAINING TO COMPETE			Strength window 2	

The Netball Performance Standards

At each stage of the LTAD pathway England Netball have produced performance standards that describe the athletic competencies required for that stage. The performance standards allow coaches to provide self-referenced feedback in terms of performance, and also enable them to devise the most appropriate programmes for athletes. Coaches are able to utilize these standards to set individual targets at each level of development, and they also provide a rigorous and transparent framework for the selection of athletes. The measurable statements of competence are divided into technical sections: a) movement skills, b) individual attacking skills, c) shooting and d) individual defensive skills. The standards also address the physiological aspects, and are broken down into a) aerobic, b) strength, c) agility, d) speed and e) core strength. Other standards are listed for psychological factors and nutrition.

KEY POINT

Performance standards are divided into the following sections:
- Movement skills
- Individual attacking skills
- Shooting
- Individual defensive skills
- Physiological aspects: a) aerobic, b) strength, c) agility, d) speed, e) core strength
- Psychological factors
- Nutrition

The Attributes of a Successful Coach

A coach must adopt a person-centred approach, which will ensure that they are flexible and sensitive to individual differences when coaching. The art of communication is not merely to convey information clearly, but for the coach to be an active listener. A coach must be honest, reliable and fair, and they should coach with enthusiasm at all times. If working at performance level the coach must be a competent decision-maker under pressure, and must demonstrate the capacity to rethink should a strategy or task fail. For the coaching process to be successful the coach must readily assess and evaluate their coaching sessions and overall training programmes. The coach is a catalyst for action, and must be determined to do the best they can for the individuals for whom they are responsible in the coaching environment.

The successful coach must be able to use a range of coaching styles in order to account for the differing learning styles within a group. Coaching styles are best described as patterns of behaviour, and also represent a range of methods used to promote learning. In netball, three approaches are advocated, and these are best described as a) tell and show, b) set up and stand back, and c) question and empower.

The effective coach will use a range of these styles, and will determine the most suitable style, given the participants' characteristics and the task to be delivered. The 'tell and show' style is often used with large groups and when safety is an issue. The 'set up and stand back' style is used to encourage learning by doing, and promotes thinking and decision-making (for example when small sided games are being played). The 'questioning' style is used with more experienced players, and the coach adopts a more facilitative role. An effective coach may deploy all of these styles in one session.

KEY POINT

- **Tell and show:** The coach uses explanations and demonstrations: players are told or shown what to do.
- **Set up and stand back:** Learning is promoted by the individual experiencing the activity. The coach should stand back and observe. This is more player-centred than the previous style.
- **Question and empower:** Uses questions to promote awareness, and encourages players to take responsibility.

To conclude, it is essential that the coach always puts the player first, and this means placing the needs of players before all other issues, such as a competition, parents, and the coach's own individual goals and ambitions. The coach should recognize individuals, and should ensure that all participants, whatever their age, ability or disability, are treated as individuals with their own specific needs, interests and goals. The coach must empower and instil self-confidence in individuals, and as a result ensure that they become responsible for their own learning and development.

PART 2
THE TECHNICAL SKILLS

CHAPTER 5

FUNDAMENTAL MOVEMENT SKILLS

Fundamental movement skills provide the backbone for the effective execution of netball specific skills, and indeed an athlete's success in netball. The movement skills are developed in the early stages of an individual's training within the fundamentals stage, but should continue to be trained and refined throughout an athlete's career. Progressive practices should initially isolate the movement aspect of any netball skill, allowing the individual an opportunity to work on their movement repertoire without the pressure of the ball being in a practice. The diagram (below) represents the movement skills of most relevance to the game of netball.

Research carried out into the positional demands and characteristics of the seven positions in relation to movement skills identified differences in movements carried out during a game. The highest percentage of sprinting was by the goal attacks and wing attacks, with the defending players

using the side step more often. The centre position spent the highest percentage of time jogging and changing the pace of the running through the court. Jumping was most common with circle players, as would be expected (goal shooter, goal attack, goal defence and goalkeeper). The difference in the movement skills executed between the seven positions highlights the need for coaches to adopt positional specific movement skill-training programmes and practices.

The Take-Off

The take-off is described as the first step required to initiate a movement, from either a moving or a stationary position. An individual will make a conscious decision to move, and it is their ability to execute this first step effectively that will maximize the speed of the response. Thus working on

this initial take-off step maximizes the chance of beating an opponent to the ball.

COACHING POINTS

- Feet shoulder-width apart.
- The opposite arm to the leg drives forwards.
- Body upright and balanced with the weight over the feet.
- Head up, looking ahead.
- High knee-lift to initiate the take-off step.

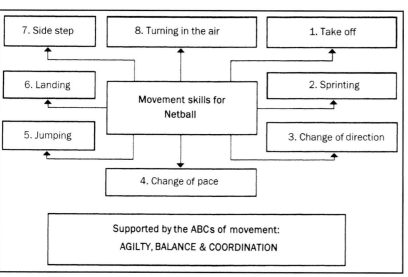

The fundamental movement skills that underpin all netball specific skills.

The take-off action.

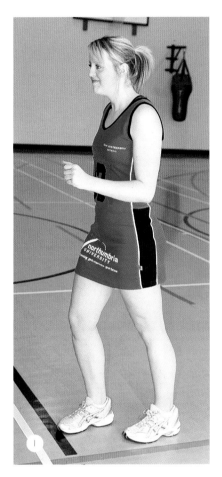

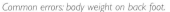

Common errors: body weight on back foot.

Here the body is too upright.

Knee lift but no transfer of weight.

Common Errors

- Knee lift is not high enough.
- Hips are not leaning forwards in the direction of the movement.
- Stepping back before going forwards.

Practices

- In twos, one partner stands behind, with the toes up to the heels of the runner. This will prevent any backward movement, and should be practised using both the left and right leg.
- The player does five quick steps on the spot, and then accelerates away in the direction called by their partner. This should be practised using the left and right leg.
- A variety of movements can be executed prior to the take-off to simulate the game, such as two-footed jumps, side step, 180-degree turn.

Sprinting

The ability to move at speed is an essential skill for netball, and the ability to change pace and direction must also be trained. Players will combine an effective take-off with a sprint to ensure they move as quickly as possible through the court when on attack and defence.

Common Errors

- Arms are not synchronized with the leg action.
- The stride length is too long, and more than a shoulder width distance.
- The knee lift is too low.

COACHING POINTS

- Keep the weight on the balls of the feet.
- Head up and upper body upright.
- The opposite arm to leg, with arms bent at 90 degrees.
- Feet shoulder-width apart.
- High knee lift.

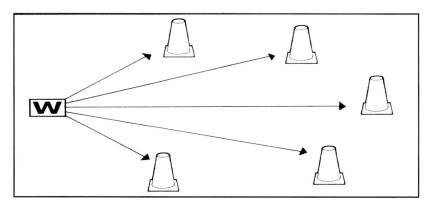

The fan sprint practice used in speed training.

The sprinting technique.

Practice

Fan sprints: Five cones are placed out at varying distances, and the worker must sprint to each cone, returning to the middle each time.

Change of Direction

A change of direction is effective when trying to deceive an opponent, and the attacker will move in one direction but then stop and cut back in another.

COACHING POINTS

- Feet shoulder-width apart.
- Weight over the feet.
- The upper body must be balanced over the feet, and upright.
- Initiate the change of direction with a strong plant of the outside foot.
- A strong push-off from the outside foot speeds up the directional change, and the inside foot leads.
- Hips and shoulders turn quickly to accelerate in the new direction.

Common Errors

- The upper body dips downwards when the foot is planted to change direction.
- A long stride is used leading into the foot plant to change direction.
- The hips are slow to turn into the direction of the movement.

Practices

- Players (minimum of six) jog around within a third of the court, and when they move into the path of another player they change direction and sprint to find a free space in the third.
- As above, but the space is reduced to half of the third area.

The change of direction.
In (2), the player in red commits the defender in one direction.
(3) shows the change of direction initiated by pushing off on the outside foot.
In (5), the attacker receives the pass on the second lead.

Change of Pace

A change of pace is often executed to displace a defender, allowing the player to receive the ball in an uncontested space. Élite performers will effectively use a moderate pace as the opponent tracks them through a space, and then suddenly accelerate to get free. A change of pace can also be accompanied with a change of direction, to effectively outwit an opponent.

COACHING POINTS

- Keep the body upright, with good body balance and alignment.
- Use small steps to allow for a sudden change of pace.
- Pump the arms to accelerate.
- Keep the weight over the feet when decreasing the pace.

Common Errors

- The stride length is too big when increasing the pace.
- Limited use of the arms when accelerating.
- The body is not balanced over the feet.
- The upper body dips when accelerating.

Practices

- Players work within a confined space and are asked to run at different speeds. The players are asked to think of the gears in a car, and to have a speed for gears three to five. On the command, players work for a period of 30sec, and change the pace according to the command. After a minute's rest, this should be repeated.
- In twos, one attacker tries to outwit the defender, and to lose them in a confined space by using a change of pace. Five attempts to lose the defender, each in a 3sec period, should be carried out, and then players rotate roles.

Jumping

Often players will jump from stationary and moving positions, which do necessitate jumping to be executed off one and two feet. Within the fundamentals stage, coaches should ensure that young performers experience and practise the five basic jumps:

- Jumping from two feet to land on two feet.
- Jumping from one foot to land on the same foot.
- Jumping from two feet to land on one foot.
- Jumping from one foot to land on the other foot.
- Jumping from one foot to land on two feet.

Netball is an aerial game, with several passes being caught in the air, and jumping is a vital movement skill for a player receiving a pass, or when defending a high ball. There is also a need for players to jump and extend forwards to take a ball at speed.

Jumping upwards.

Jumping forwards.

COACHING POINTS FOR JUMPING UPWARDS

- Use a two-footed base where possible.
- Feet shoulder-width apart.
- Lower the hips but keep the body upright.
- Arms swing back and vigorously upwards.
- Maintain a straight body position in the air.

COACHING POINTS FOR JUMPING FORWARDS

- Bend the knees, lower the hips, but keep the body upright.
- Swing the arms, lowering and driving the body forwards.
- Keep the head up.

Common Errors

- Limited arm movement in the direction of the jump.
- The hips do not lower sufficiently for the upward jump.
- The knees are not flexed on take-off.

Landing

The ability to land is an essential skill required to accompany a jump, particularly when considering the footwork rule applied in netball. Landing effectively is crucial in terms of preventing injury, and a coach will always spend a great deal of time on developing this technique.

Common Errors

- Landing on the heels, or flat footed.
- Not flexing the knees.
- Body leaning forwards over the feet.

COACHING POINTS

- Flex the knees, and slightly flex the ankles on impact.
- Land on the balls of the feet.
- Keep the upper body upright, the abdominals tight and the head upright.
- If landing on one foot, bring the other down as quickly as possible to ensure balance and control.

Practices for Jumping and Landing

- The **cone jump**: scatter cones in a third of the court: the player jogs to any cone, then accelerates and sprints to another. As the second cone is reached, the player jumps over in a forward direction, using either the right or left foot to take off (coach encourages the player to try a different take-off foot each time).

- The above practice can be adapted, and when a player moves to a red cone they jump forwards, but when they reach a green cone they jump upwards.

The Side Step

Using a side step is an essential movement skill that will enhance a player's ability to get free, move around, and also track an opponent when defending. Side-stepping will allow circle players to move in various directions in an attempt to outwit an opponent within a confined space. Defending through all areas of the court involves tracking a player from in front, and often the lateral movement means a side step may be used.

Common Errors

- Feet beyond shoulder-width apart.
- The weight falls over the outside foot.

COACHING POINTS

- Keep on the balls of the feet.
- Head up.
- Keep the knees slightly flexed with the trunk upright.
- The feet should remain shoulder-width apart.
- The weight should be balanced over the feet.

Practices

- A worker is positioned in the centre of a grid, which has a coloured cone in each corner. As a colour is called, the player must side step out to the cone and return to the centre.
- In fours, two players are outside the circle, positioned on either side. An attacker and a defender are in the shooting circle. Using side steps to move around the attacker, the defender must ensure that she is ball side.

The side step. In (2), keep the weight on the balls of the feet and look ahead. In (4), the player pushes off on the outside foot on the sidestep to change direction.

Turning in the air.

Turning in the Air

Jumping and landing are the essential skills supporting the ability to turn in the air. A player will use a turn in the air to ensure that on landing they face the direction of play and the attacking goal. The ball carrier in netball has only three seconds to make a decision and pass or shoot. If a player can jump and turn in the air before landing, this will allow more time to observe the options available and make the appropriate decision. Turning in the air removes the need to pivot after landing to face the direction of play.

Common Error

- Not turning the hips after take-off, and initiating the turn early.

Practices

- Two static throwers (T1 and T2) with one worker (W). The worker moves to the right to receive a pass from T1, and passes to T2, and this is repeated from T2. The worker varies their movement to receive (left and right side).
- As above, but the throwers vary their passes – either flat, high, inside or outside the worker. The worker chooses which way to turn, based on the pass.

Summary

The movement skills outlined in this section will support the development of all the specific skills required in netball. The ability to move efficiently requires effective technique, together with the required level of fitness. All the movement skills outlined require good physical conditioning, and players must work hard to ensure they are fast, strong and powerful.

COACHING POINTS

- Use the coaching points for jumping.
- After take-off, begin to initiate the turn with the head, shoulders and hips turning.
- Keep the body upright; the abdominals should be tight.
- Maintain the balanced body position on landing.

CHAPTER 6

INDIVIDUAL NETBALL SKILLS

Netball is physiologically demanding, and players must exercise a high level of skill, performing passing, catching and shooting skills in an ever-changing tactical and pressurized environment. An individual must also be able to make accurate decisions in terms of when, where and why a particular skill is executed. For example, what type of pass will be best to use in this situation? How will you decide when to release the ball? What are your passing options?

This chapter will present an overview of the following skills:
- catching (two-handed and one-handed)
- chest pass
- bounce pass
- shoulder pass
- overhead pass
- shooting

Catching

For the static two-handed catch a player must prepare to catch by keeping their eyes on the ball, moving their body to meet the ball, and extending the arms to reach towards the ball.

At the execution phase of the catch the player must have their fingers spread around the back and sides of the ball, and must squeeze on to it. The thumbs are in the middle, and with the first fingers ensure a 'W' shape behind the ball. The hands and arms 'give' on contact, and the ball is brought into the body in preparation to throw.

KEY COACHING POINTS FOR CATCHING

- Eyes on the ball.
- Fingers spread.
- 'W' shape with thumbs and first fingers behind the ball.
- 'Give' on contact with the arms and hands.

The 'W' behind the ball. (Reproduced by courtesy of England Netball)

The two-handed catch.

Catching and turning in the air.

The one-handed catch.

When catching a ball two-handed on the move, a player must also keep their head up and jump to catch in order to control the momentum. A player must land in a balanced position with their weight over the landing foot or both feet. The hips should be lowered and the knees flexed to provide more stability and control to the landing position.

Often a player will catch the ball and turn simultaneously in the air so they face the direction of play. This means they do not need to pivot after landing, and therefore have more time to process information and make a decision of who to pass to. For this to be executed correctly a player must drive up and extend towards the ball with the feet off the ground, ensuring that the turn begins at the take-off point. To initiate the turn the player must take off by pushing in the direction of the turn, and should move their head, shoulders and hips in the intended direction.

On occasions within the game there is a need to catch one-handed, particularly if the ball is out to the side of the body and at a greater distance away from the body. A player will extend their catching arm and hand towards the ball, and as soon as possible they will add the second hand as the ball is brought into the body. A player must also 'give' when catching to absorb the impact. The ball is controlled by the fingers being spread around the ball. A coach should ensure that players develop the ability to catch one-handed with both the right and left hand.

Throwing

Any player must develop their throwing skills by developing competence in the full range of throws. A throw is only successful in the game if the ball carrier has made the correct decision and addresses the many perceptual factors.

For the successful execution of all throws there are some common coaching points that should be stressed to any player. A player should always keep their eyes on the target, keep their body balanced throughout the pass, and also

follow through with the arms and hands towards the target.

The Chest Pass

The chest pass is most commonly used over shorter distances when a defender is not between the ball carrier and the receiver. This pass allows the player to send a flat and fast pass that is easily controlled. The pass starts from the two-handed catching position, with the ball

The chest pass. (Reproduced by courtesy of England Netball)

held at chest height. In the preparation phase the fingers must be spread behind the ball, keeping the elbows low and relaxed. In the execution phase the bodyweight is transferred forwards, and

KEY COACHING POINTS

- The ball is held at chest height.
- The elbows are low and relaxed.
- Maintain the 'W' shape used when catching.
- Transfer the bodyweight forwards when throwing.
- Extend the arms and wrists on the follow-through.

the ball is released as the arms and wrists extend. A player must follow through with their hands, fingers and arms.

The Bounce Pass

The two-handed bounce pass is used over short distances and is most commonly used by players when passing to someone in a confined space, for example a wing attack or centre passing on the circle edge to a shooter inside the shooting circle. This type of pass works effectively against tall defence who have strength in their ability to intercept and challenge any aerial ball being sent to a shooter. In the preparation

phase the ball is held just below chest height and the player applies a similar action to the chest pass. In the execution phase the ball should bounce two-thirds of the distance between the ball carrier and the receiver, the bounce often being kept low to prevent a defender intercepting the pass.

On occasions a one-handed bounce pass is used, which enables the player to obtain a better angle for the pass and also to protect the ball from a defender. In the preparation phase the ball is taken to the side of the body and kept at waist height. To execute the one-handed pass the player takes a step across with the opposite foot to the throwing arm.

The bounce pass. (Reproduced by courtesy of England Netball)

The shoulder pass. (Reproduced by courtesy of England Netball)

The Shoulder Pass

This pass is used over longer distances and requires considerable power. In the preparation phase the ball carrier takes up a balanced starting position with the opposite foot forwards in relation to the throwing arm. The ball is positioned just

The one-handed bounce pass. (Reproduced by courtesy of England Netball)

KEY COACHING POINTS

- The ball is held above and behind the shoulder.
- The opposite foot to the throwing arm is placed forwards.
- As the ball is released, the hips rotate.
- On execution the hand, arm and shoulder extend forwards.

above the shoulder with the fingers spread behind the ball. A young or novice player may use the second hand to steady the ball prior to executing the pass. The ball is positioned behind the shoulder to ensure that maximum power is gained. As the ball is released the hips rotate as the hand, arm and shoulder move forwards towards the receiver. The bodyweight is transferred forwards in the direction of the pass and on to the front foot. In the follow-through the arm, hand and fingers extend towards the target.

The Overhead Pass

This pass allows the ball carrier to clear a defender's reach, and the overhead pass can be high, floating or straight. The ball is held above the head, and the position of

The overhead pass. (Reproduced by courtesy of England Netball)

release technique that now dominates the game. It must be noted that the Caribbean nations follow the technique implemented by Trinidadian shooter Jean Pierre, who played at international level and competed in five consecutive world championships. In this Caribbean style the shooting arm starts much lower than in the Australian style, but is released at a similar point. The stance is different, with the Caribbean shot having the shooting foot placed forwards with the weight on the back foot, in contrast to the stance being parallel with the feet a shoulder-width apart.

However, it is the Australian high release shot that is adopted and coached within the development and international programmes in the UK. This style allows a shooter to clear the ball away from a defender. In the preparation phase the shooter should note the following technical points:

- Body should be balanced, with feet a hip-width apart and the back straight.
- The ball is held high above the head, with the ball resting on the fingers of the shooting hand.
- The wrist under the ball and fingers should face backwards.
- The second hand is used to steady the ball by its positioning on the side of the ball.
- Eyes focused on the front of the ring, and ball to be lifted above this point.

At the execution phase:
- Wrist should drop slightly behind the head.
- Use the index finger to guide the shot with a little backspin.
- Use knees and ankles to push ball upwards and forwards to goal.
- The ball should lift high over the front of the ring and for a clean shot should begin to drop into the goal at the midpoint above the ring.
- In the follow-through the index finger should point forwards and slightly downwards.

A shooter may use their footwork skills, and may use the rules to their own advantage by implementing a step

the fingers and hands is the same as the two-handed catch. The ball is taken slightly behind the head, with the wrists extended backwards in the preparation phase. As the ball is released, the arms extend to propel the ball forwards to the receiver. The power for this throw is from the elbows as the arm extends.

Shooting

There are several shooting styles across the world, and the preferred techniques have changed from a two-handed shot to the one-handed high release shot. Australian shooting legend Margaret Caldow devised the one-handed high

The shooting action. (Reproduced by courtesy of England Netball)

backwards, forwards or to the side when in the act of shooting. If a defender is placing a great deal of pressure on the shooter, the step backwards and to the side can counteract this pressure, and give the shooter more space to release the ball. Such steps can also be used when throwing the ball to relieve pressure being forced on you by the defender, and can gain you an advantage.

The step forwards is used when the defender is not positioned in front of you, allowing you the chance to move closer to the post. This is most commonly seen in a penalty shot situation when your opponent is stood by your side until the ball is released.

Once the basic shooting technique has been mastered, then a player can begin to use the step. When executing the step it is vital that the bodyweight is rebalanced over the foot you have stepped on. Balance must be maintained throughout the action and follow-through.

Netball rules permit only two players to shoot in a match, these being the goal attack and the goal shooter; hence it is vital that they have a high percentage success rate. A shooter must have confidence in their ability, and must have the qualities to cope well under pressure.

Shooting with a step back.
(Reproduced by courtesy of England Netball)

Shooting with a step to the side.
(Reproduced by courtesy of England Netball)

TIPS FOR SHOOTING

- Follow the Australian technique.
- Master the technique by practising daily.
- Body balance is crucial.
- Use the stepping techniques to gain an advantage.
- Remember your landing foot when using the step techniques.

CHAPTER 7

ATTACKING SKILLS

The methods that are utilized by a player to get free, draw upon several movement skills outlined in Chapter 5. A player must be able to get free from a stationary and moving position within the game, using their vision and powers of decision-making to identify a suitable front or back space to move into. The experienced performer will be autonomous in their execution of the skills, and would be able to demonstrate the ability to vary the attacking skills used according to the tactical and technical strengths and weaknesses of the opposition. In game conditions a player must also be able to read the necessary cues around them, work to get free under pressure, and ultimately execute a well timed move into the available free space.

It is vital that a coach offers practices that work to enhance a player's decision-making powers, and this can be achieved by adding the perceptual factors into the training programme.

Contesting as a wing attack.

The attacking skills can often incorporate one or more of the following movement skills: sprinting, changes of pace and direction. The sprint to receive the ball is commonly referred to as a 'lead'. Some of the most important methods used to get free are these:

- straight and diagonal lead
- double lead
- dodge and double dodge
- protecting a space

The Straight and Diagonal Lead

The correct sprinting technique is applied to this attacking move, and the player must focus ahead on the ball and the available space. The initial take-off is important, and the attacker must use a high knee lift to gain momentum to move away from the defender. The direction of the lead is dependent upon the position of the defender(s), and should the defence mark from a side position, then the player will often execute a diagonal move. Often defence will mark from the 'in front' position, and a player may then decide to lead to the back space (either diagonally or straight).

A player must practise the diagonal lead from both sides, and in a forwards and backwards direction. It is also important to practise this lead by taking off on the inside and outside foot: the outside foot take-off allows the attacker to drive out quickly on the diagonal and away from the defender; the inside foot take-off allows the attacker to cut off the movement path of the defender.

The Double Lead

A double lead is executed if on the first lead the ball has not been received. A double lead often combines the attacking sprint with a change of direction, and can be used to commit a defender in one direction before moving into a free space. This lead requires a convincing body movement, and is often effective when the defender is persistent and marking tightly one on one. The change of direction after the first lead, if executed quickly, ultimately leaves the defender out of position and opens up a space to receive the pass in.

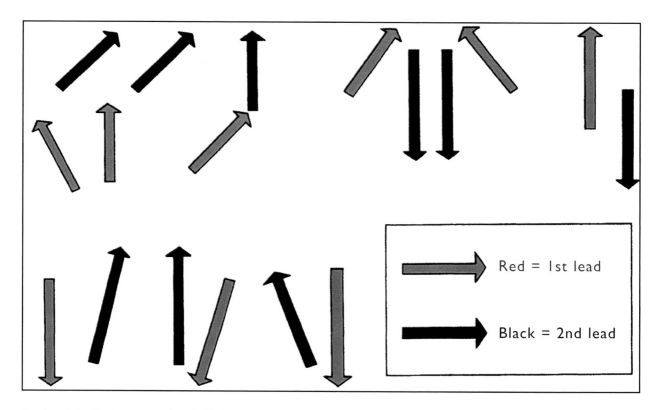

A variety of directional movements for a double lead.

The reverse pivot.

The double lead can be executed in a number of combined directions, some of which are illustrated on the previous page.

The various combinations open up the forward or back space for the attacker, and the up and back lead combination is useful when the defender has maintained a strong defensive position, as the attacker has moved up the court. This move can also open up space when there is a potentially crowded situation. The change of direction at the end of the first lead must be implemented when the ball carrier is ready to release the ball. If

KEY COACHING POINTS FOR THE REVERSE PIVOT

- On the balls of the feet.
- Step to the right using the left leg across the body (moving to the right).
- Reverse the feet for pivoting in the opposite direction.
- Pivot on the right foot.
- Turn the head and shoulders quickly.
- Regain focus quickly on the new direction of movement.

moving backwards, the attacker must maintain their vision on the ball in order to monitor the flight and to time the jump to receive.

When using a double lead to get free, a player may use the reverse pivot to change direction and this is effective when a defender is marking closely in the front position.

The reverse pivot involves the attacker turning out and away from the defender marking them and is often used to outwit a tight man-to-man defender. The reverse pivot is illustrated above.

The dodge.

The Dodge and Double Dodge

The dodge can be used to free an opponent, and is often executed when the defender is marking very tightly one on one, and often from an 'in front' position. The dodge demands that the attacker executes a feint movement in one direction – often stated as 'selling a dummy to the defender' – before moving in another direction. This method is often used by players to get free from a stationary position, and demands a good, balanced body position. The attacker feints a movement to one side by planting the foot and using an upper body movement by the leading shoulder, before moving off in the other direction. The feint must be strong and convincing, without the attacker shifting all the bodyweight in the direction of this first move. A powerful turn of the hips will initiate a fast movement into another direction to find a free space.

A double dodge can be executed, which involves two feint movements to commit the defender. This is useful when the attacker has not deceived the defender on the first feint, and may need to use another feint to free themselves from the opponent.

Protecting a Space

There are instances in the game where an attacker may wish to protect a space to receive the ball, rather than execute a lead or dodge. This is most commonly seen within the goal circle where a shooter works to hold the position by making slight adjustments with the feet to ensure they keep the defender away from the space. The attacker must maintain a strong body position, with knees flexed and a base slightly wider than shoulder width to maintain stability. Timing of the move to receive is critical in this skill, and the ball carrier will have released the ball before the attacker makes the move.

The attacker will hold the position up close to the defender until the last possible moment, and will then either lunge, jump or reach to receive the ball, keeping themselves between the ball and the defender. The pass must be accurate, and consideration should be given to the strengths of the defender in order to decide which pass is the most effective. A defender who has good elevation and intercepts well in the air would be restricted by a bounce pass being placed into the space.

Whilst in possession, any team must work to provide at least two forward and one square option. Attackers will apply the relevant method of getting free, following evaluation of their opponents' strengths and the space available. The attacking move executed can split the defenders and free up space for a fellow team mate to receive the ball. This does mean there could be up to three players moving and attempting to get free, and these players must have good vision to ensure that they offer for the ball in a different space. Communication and team work is therefore essential between players, and the **SPACE** principles described (right) will support a player in using their attacking skills to best effect in a game.

TOP TIPS

- **S**can the area for important cues.
- **P**layer at the front initiates.
- **A**lert to all players' intentions.
- **C**learing space for team mates, and maintain court balance.
- **E**xecution of the pass, and a well timed movement.

Holding space.

The bounce pass to a shooter from the circle edge.

CHAPTER 8

DEFENDING SKILLS

Each of the seven players on the court is required to defend, and each must be able to demonstrate the ability to defend both on the receiver and on the ball. When marking the receiver, the defender must shadow the attacker and restrict and prevent them from moving into the desirable space.

When defending on the ball a player can influence the accuracy, direction, pace and height of the pass. By placing pressure on the ball, the defender should limit the options by restricting the ball carrier's vision to locate the mover and passing space.

In netball there are three stages of defence whereby a player makes attempts to gain an interception. When defending, a player should make a quick transition from one stage to the next: for example, one on one marking – pressure on the ball – restricts the player. At all times the player is trying to gain possession by forcing the receiver or ball carrier into an error.

STAGES OF DEFENCE

Stage 1   Marking a player without the ball.
Stage 2   Marking a player in possession of the ball.
Stage 3   Restricting the player movement.

Stage One Defence

The aim of stage one defence is to mark a player closely to prevent them from receiving the ball, or to gain an interception. If the ball is moving down the court, a defender must constantly

Stage one defending.

KEY COACHING POINTS

- Feet shoulder-width apart.
- Weight balanced on the balls of the feet.
- Arms flexed at the front or side of the body.
- Head up.
- Watch player and ball with your back to the player.
- Position within an arm's reach of the attacker.
- Defender half covers the attacking player.
- Body is slightly angled to the player's uncovered side.

move around their opponent and reposition as the ball switches from side to side. The defender tries to ensure that their opponent is not an option for the ball carrier.

When a player is moving to get free from a dead ball situation – for example, a centre pass or throw-in – the defender must shadow the attacker and position very close to this player. The defender in this stage will try to intercept, force an uncontrolled receipt of the ball, or force an out-of-court. Positioning on the front of an opponent is advantageous and forces a lofted ball to the back space.

Stage Two Defence

If an opponent receives the ball, the defender must then put pressure on the ball carrier and mark the pass from a distance of 0.9m from the attacker's landing foot. Defenders will at times drop back from 0.9m to cover the immediate space near to the ball carrier. Therefore, the aim of stage two is to apply pressure and restrict the vision of the ball carrier. The defender will try to intercept the pass, to tip the ball or force a weak pass.

There are two approaches within this stage, and a defender must decide whether to a) keep their feet on the ground, and

The approaches to stage two defending – feet down.

The approaches to stage two defending – with a jump.

cover the ball and space with their outstretched arms and hands; or b) cover the ball but prepare to jump when the ball is released from the thrower. A defender who has good elevation and a well timed jump will use approach b) to try for an interception. Circle defence will often use a combination of both approaches to try and force the shooters into making an error, whilst players defending through the court will prefer to keep their feet grounded so they can recover and deny space should they not gain possession. A defender must read the cues from the passer, and assess the best approach to implement by asking themselves the following questions:

- Is my opponent taller than me?
- Does my opponent release the ball from a low position?
- If I am unsuccessful in stage two, can my player gain ground away from me and be a key option for her team?
- Does the shooter miss when I lean, or when I jump?
- If I defend further back from 0.9m, does this force a slower pass for my team mates to intercept?

The defender should influence the direction and height of the pass if an interception cannot be gained, and this may allow an interception for a defender marking the receiver. Following an assessment of their opponent, a defender will select the best arm position to cover the ball, the distance they should stand from their opponent, and their shoulder/body alignment in relation to the ball carrier and receiver.

Stage Three Defence

This stage is also known as restrictive marking, and the aim is to prevent an opponent from moving to their desired space on the court. A successful stage three defender will ensure that the player does not have the freedom to move to a desired location, and will also force them to a sideline and into a crowded space. If a defender can restrict the attacker and keep them away from ball side, they will force the opposition to use diagonal passes, which are more easily intercepted. If a defender is not successful at stage two, they must quickly recover and ensure that they close down the space.

A defender must have good agility, and use small running and shuffling steps to track and stay close to the player in this stage. The defender should angle their body to drive the player away from the key attacking space. After stage two the defender will be facing the player and not the ball, so it is vital that after momentarily delaying the run of the attacker, they turn to face the ball.

Stage three defending.

Throughout each stage of defending the player is striving to gain an interception, and for this to occur a player must make a judgement as to the correct time to take off for the intercept. Players should always seek opportunities to try for an interception, and with good timing the frequency of a successful turnover will increase. The defender must develop good vision in order to mark an opponent, but must also be aware of the path of the ball, and seek out an intercepting opportunity. This intercepting opportunity may require the player to drop off their own opponent and possibly move to another opponent or space. Deception on defence can trick the opposition into thinking that there is an attacking option not covered by the defender, and by positioning away from the space and the opponent the defender makes a move for the interception.

Stage three defending.

PART 3
NETBALL TACTICS

CHAPTER 9

NETBALL GAME PRINCIPLES

It is well acknowledged that the game of netball is multifaceted, and to support the development of a player, coach or umpire, a set of principles have been identified and documented. In order to apply the principles in the game, a player must demonstrate that they can execute the technical skills (movement skills, ball skills), and they must be effective in their decision making. The principles therefore cover the technical and tactical aspects of netball, which are divided into attacking and defensive components. A set of attacking and defensive principles are documented here to provide a framework for the development of a player.

Attacking Principles

Goal Scoring

The ultimate aim of a game is to score a goal, and in netball there are only two playing positions that can do this: goal shooter and goal attack. The two shooters in the game must be able to shoot under pressure, and when they are being defended (in the modified games of high five and first step netball the shooter is not defended). Players need time to practise in training sessions, and should try and execute a movement to receive the ball in a prime shooting position, which is nearer to the post. A coach should allow all players the opportunity to learn to play one of the shooting positions, and should coach them the high shooting technique (see Chapter 6, p. 42).

Providing Options for the Ball Carrier

There should always be three passing options available to the ball carrier, and it is often a preference to have two forward options and a square option available. The ball carrier must make the correct decision regarding who they will pass to, based upon the position of the defenders, the space available, and the timing of the mover to receive (if too early or too late this could affect the successful receipt of the pass).

Gaining the Ball Side Position

The receiver should ensure that they remain between the ball carrier and their opponent, as it is harder for a defender to intercept in this situation. The ball carrier can pass the ball faster and more directly into the hands of the receiver in this instance.

A1 = Attacker 1 with ball
A2 = Attacker 2
A3 = Attacker 3
A4 = Attacker 4

Giving a ball carrier choices.

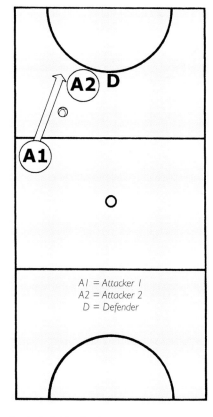

A1 = Attacker 1
A2 = Attacker 2
D = Defender

Staying ball side of a player.

Passing on the Straight Line

This is the most direct route from the ball carrier to the receiver, and it is also the fastest route to goal. By passing on the straight line there is less of an angle for the defenders to intercept. A diagonal ball allows more time for a defender to position themselves, and to move into the line of the pass for the interception.

Using a Square Pass

If the forward options are not available to the ball carrier, then there should be an option to pass the ball square to a player moving from behind. This ensures that the

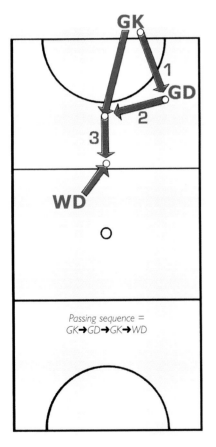

Using a square pass to GK on the overlap run.

attacking players in front of the ball carrier are not drawn up the court so as to cause problems with subsequent passes to goal. This square pass can also open up the court, and the width available to the attacking team.

Space Principles

All players in the game must recognize the space principles in order to create space for themselves and others. Defenders will try to restrict the space available and therefore make attempts to disrupt play.

All players must be able to scan the area for important cues, and as the ball is caught, the ball carrier should observe the position of the defenders in relation to her team mates. The ball carrier should have established who is quicker on the court by assessing who is getting free from their opponent more easily.

The player at the front of the attack cannot see what is happening behind, and so the players behind the front attacker 'have the eyes' to see all movements. It is therefore the responsibility of the front player to make the first move, and subsequently the player at the back will move to a different area.

The ball carrier should be alert to the players' intentions by looking at who is indicating for the ball, or who is timing their move accurately.

To achieve an effective attacking play and to use the space available, there is a need to balance the court. If the attacking players can do this they will be providing more than one option for the ball carrier by creating space for themselves, or for others in their team, to use. The following observations will help a player develop an understanding of court balance:

- If there are two players moving in the same space to take a pass, the court could not have been balanced.
- The ball should travel in straight lines (not diagonals across the court).
- A player must often lead a defender out of the main space to receive the ball, or allow a team mate to receive the ball.

- A ball carrier must turn to face the direction of play to sight passing options early.
- The pass should be delivered in the space ahead of the receiver.
- The receiver must time their movement so they receive on the straight line.

Players may also interchange positions in order to create an effective attack, and this is where two players change their position and role on the court. Thus when the court is balanced, two attacking players may interchange roles: for example, the goal attack may drop into the shooting circle, and the goal shooter may move out and become involved in the play within the attacking third.

A second example of an interchange is between the wing attack and centre positions: the wing attack will move up the court and link with the defending players, which is normally the role of the centre, who at this point has dropped to play the wing attack role. This can allow the centre to have a break in the amount of work they do in the mid-court, but it can also disrupt a strong mid-court defence.

SPACE PRINCIPLES

- Scan the area for important cues.
- The player at the front initiates.
- Be alert to all players' intentions.
- Clear space for team mates and maintain court balance.
- Ensure the execution of the pass and a well timed movement.

Defending Principles

Gaining Possession

A team can only score goals by regaining possession, and the defending team must ensure that they make every attempt to gain an interception, to force the opposition into error or to rebound a missed shot.

Gaining the Ball Side Position

The defender must strive to gain the ball side position, which means being between the ball carrier and their opponent. In this position the ball carrier is often forced to send a higher trajectory pass, allowing more time for a defender to move into the path of the ball and intercept.

Applying Pressure on the Attacking Players

The defending players must apply sufficient pressure on the attacking players to force an error and ultimately to regain possession. The defenders will be striving to gain an interception, otherwise known as a turnover. The three stages of defence must be applied successfully by all members of the team to ensure pressure is placed upon the ball carrier and potential receivers of the next pass.

Reducing the Ball Carrier's Options

The attacking team will try and provide choices for the ball carrier, and it is the defence who must try and counteract this. By reducing the options available there is a chance that the ball carrier will make a passing error, or will hold the ball for more than 3sec. The defending players should communicate with each other to ensure all passing options are closed down, and that the space for the attacking players to move into is also limited. The defender should close off any options on the straight line, and try and force a longer diagonal pass that is more challenging for the ball carrier to execute, and often more easily intercepted.

Restricting the Attacking Players' Space

The defender should work hard to force the attacking player into a difficult area to receive the pass: for example, close to a side- or backline, or near a third line which is the boundary for an area they are not able to move into. Closing down the space can be achieved by the defence marking the receivers on the ball side, and also by the defender marking the ball carrier. The latter should defend at the correct distance, but be angled to cover the space on the straight line. Once again, the back defenders should communicate to the defender marking the ball carrier to ensure that the correct position is adopted for the stage two defence to close off the available options.

CHAPTER 10

APPLYING THE PRINCIPLES IN ATTACK

The Centre Pass

In the game of netball the centre pass starts the game, and alternates between teams after each goal is scored. Both teams therefore have an equal opportunity to score goals from the centre pass. The attacking team must practise a variety of set-ups for the centre pass, and ensure that all team members know the options within each of the set-ups. The centre taking the pass should know which options will be available in a specific set-up, and select the most appropriate given the position of the defenders, the available space, and the timing of the receiver.

Ideally the wing attack should take a high percentage of passes at the first phase of the centre pass, but all teams should work with all four positions (GA, WA, GD and WD) to add variety to the attacking play. The wing attack should communicate with the goal attack to know who should receive each of the forward centre passes. Goal defence and wing defence are available as support players at the centre pass, and occasionally teams will relieve pressure on the attacking players and put a pass back to

one of these defence players. The success of each centre pass should be calculated, and teams should make adjustments to their patterns of play from the centre pass, having assessed the strengths and weaknesses of the opposition.

All players moving to receive at the centre pass must demonstrate effective movement skills, and use strong and efficient footwork to move into the centre third at speed. The player receiving the first pass should turn fully to locate the

straight line options, and if limited, this player will rely on the square pass to the player moving on the overlap run. If a player is not used during the centre pass they must reposition, and be an option in the forthcoming passages of play.

The following centre pass options demonstrate the straight line principle, and limit the chances of an interception by the defence:

- The wing attack sprints out and receives the ball centrally from the centre.

KEY POINTS

- Each centre pass set-up has more than one passing option.
- Players must communicate, for example goal attack and wing attack.
- A player must react quickly, and execute movement skills at speed.
- Always turn fully to face forwards after receiving the centre pass.
- Avoid over-using one player.
- Vary the centre pass set-up to outwit the defenders.

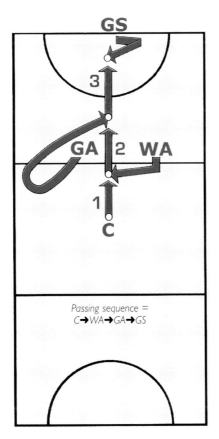

Passing sequence =
C➔WA➔GA➔GS

The straight line principle at the centre pass.

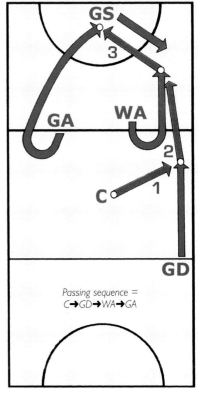

Passing sequence =
C➔GD➔WA➔GA

Centre pass to the goal defence.

- Goal attack offers at the centre pass, but then drops towards the circle edge for the next pass.
- Goal shooter carries out a double lead back to the post for the third pass

- The centre pass is given on the overlap to the goal defence.
- The wing attack leads out for the first pass, but then drops back to receive a lifted ball from the goal defence towards the circle edge.
- Goal shooter leads out of the circle to open up the space for the goal attack, and the wing attack can fake a pass to the goal shooter, but pass to the goal attack.

- The wing attack positions on the goal attack side, and takes the first pass.
- The goal attack leads over the

transverse line at the centre pass, but then drops back (also an option).
- Goal shooter leads out of the circle to receive the second pass.
- Goal attack moves into the circle at speed to receive the ball in a shooting position.

There may be times in a game where additional tactics need to be applied by the players on the transverse line in order to free themselves from their opponent. The wing attack and goal attack may use either a screen or an interchange of position to outwit the defending players.

The Screen

- The wing attack uses the goal attack side as a screen, and receives the first pass.

- The goal attack moves over the transverse line, but quickly drops back to receive the second pass from the wing attack.
- The goal shooter has moved to the top of the circle, but then drops back to receive a pass from the goal attack.
- Passing to the goal defence and wing defence are also options for the centre.
- The goal defence can also screen for the wing defence.
- The wing attack and goal attack both pull the two defence forwards, and then drop back.
- The wing attack receives the second pass on the straight line.
- The goal shooter then receives the third pass.
- The goal attack and centre are both options for the third pass also.

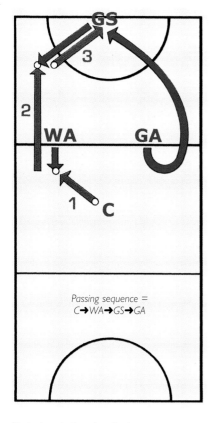

Centre pass to the wing attack.

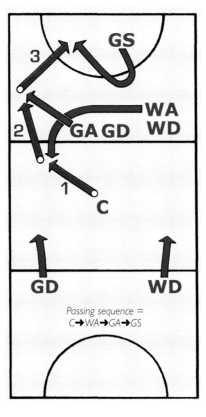

A screen at the centre pass.

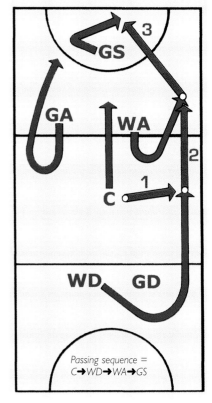

A screen set by the goal defence at the centre pass.

The Interchange

- Here the goal attack and wing attack set up in a 'stack' position on the transverse line.
- The wing attack interchanges space and side with the goal attack to receive the centre pass.
- The goal shooter offers a straight line option for the second pass.
- If the goal shooter is not free, the ball could be played back to the centre on a double play.
- The goal attack has moved wide, and sprints into the circle for the third pass.
- This centre pass involves the goal defence and wing defence interchanging (scissor movement).
- The wing defence receives the centre pass, and passes on the straight line to the goal attack, who has also interchanged spaces with the wing attack. The pass could go to the goal defence, who then uses the wing attack on the straight line pass.
- Options for the third pass could be a pass to the wing attack at the top of the circle, or a pass to the goal shooter who is sprinting towards the post to receive.

Players must ensure that they balance the court at all times, and two players should not be in the same area of the court at the centre pass. The ball carrier must be provided with more than one option at all times: the illustrations (below) show an example of one of the options available.

Goal-Line Throw-In

When a team regains possession in their opponents' attacking end, there is a need to set up quickly and move the ball as fast as possible. The defending unit can therefore initiate an effective attacking

> **THE PRINCIPLES OF ATTACKING PLAY**
>
> - Balance the court.
> - More than one option.
> - Use of the straight line.
> - Use the overlap for the square pass.
> - Defence players (goal keeper, goal defence and wing defence) should move the ball through to the centre third.
> - There should always be a back-up option.

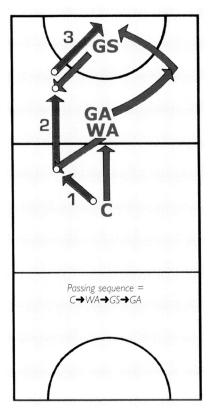

Passing sequence =
C➜WA➜GS➜GA

The interchange.

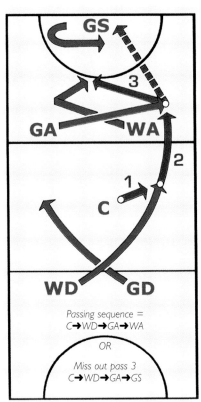

Passing sequence =
C➜WD➜GA➜WA

OR

Miss out pass 3
C➜WD➜GA➜GS

The interchange by the goal defence and wing defence.

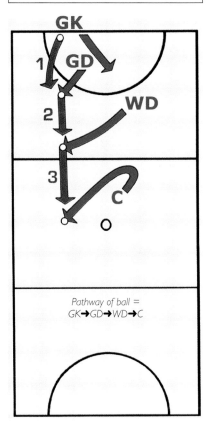

Pathway of ball =
GK➜GD➜WD➜C

A goal-line throw-in received by the goal defence.

strategy if they can react quickly at the throw-in and move the ball through to the mid-court to link with the attacking unit. The goal keeper will tend to take the goal-line throw-in, but teams do not always want to be predictable, and often the goal defence can be seen taking the throw-in from the goal line. The principles of attacking play outlined should be adhered to, and are summarized in the 'Key Points' box on the previous page.

- The goal defence positions close to the goal keeper, and then drops back to receive a high ball.
- The wing defence has positioned ball side of their opponent on the top of the circle edge, and moves up the court to receive the second pass (the goal keeper also moves, to support and to be an option for a square pass).

- The centre executes a double lead to receive the third pass.
- The ball carrier must always be the support player, and move to provide a square option (see diagram on previous page).
- Wing defence moves to the top of the circle to receive a pass from the goal keeper (see below left).
- The goal defence and wing defence are options, to open up the space in either of the outside channels.
- For variety, the centre provides an option on the straight line, but this should not be used on many occasions as it draws the centre up too far.
- If the centre gets the ball, the wing defence may interchange and provide an option in the mid-court area.
- The three channels of the court are filled, and court balance is achieved.

Sideline Throw-In

At the throw-in there should be three options available to the ball carrier, and these should be over varying distances from the thrower. After the ball has been released, the ball carrier should provide a square option; this serves as the back-up and support if the ball cannot travel forwards. The wing defence would normally take the throw-in within the centre third, and teams will have their own preference for a sideline throw-in in their defending third – but it is usually the goal defence or wing defence. Using the goal keeper on a sideline throw-in can expose the shooting circle, and should the ball be intercepted there is likely to be the goal shooter free in a prime shooting position.

A Sideline Throw-In from the Centre Third

- Wing defence takes the throw-in, and centre receives the first pass.
- Wing attack is ball side of her opponent, and moves for the second pass on the straight line.
- Goal attack clears, and then leads for the ball on the top of the circle edge.
- Goal shooter then receives the ball leading towards the post.
- Goal defence provides the back-up should the forward options not be possible.
- The centre would be on the circle edge as another option for the third pass.

A Sideline Throw-In from the Attacking Third

- Wing attack passes the ball to centre, who drives to the circle edge.
- The pass could go to the goal shooter, with the centre placing herself at the top of the circle edge.

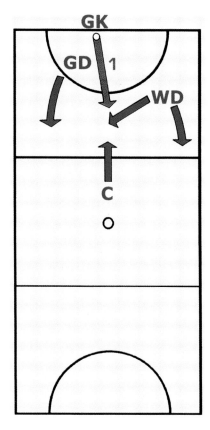

A throw-in received by the wing defence.

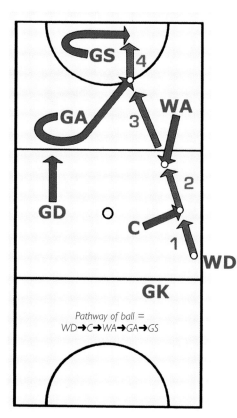

Pathway of ball =
WD➔C➔WA➔GA➔GS

A sideline throw-in from the centre third.

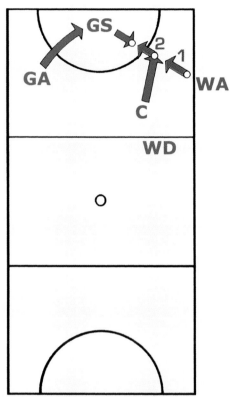

A sideline throw-in from the attacking third.

The WD supports the attack and a double play occurs.

- Wing defence provides the back-up for the wing attack.
- Goal shooter receives the second pass on a short passing option.
- Goal attack could receive the third pass under the post, depending on the location of the defender; but the goal shooter may want to shoot.
- The goal shooter could also use the centre for the next pass, and receive it back nearer the post (see diagram above).
- Wing attack passes to the wing defence to open up the court space, and executes a double play to take the ball on the edge of the circle (above right).
- Goal attack and goal shooter are both in the circle, and the goal attack rotates and clears to allow the pass to go to the goal shooter.
- This is a good option if the centre is unable to position ball side.

Full Court Systems

The following illustrations offer some examples of full court systems to represent the transition of the ball from the defending to the attacking end of the court. At all times there must be two

KEY POINTS

- A team should add variety at the throw-in and not be predictable.
- There should always be three options available to the ball carrier.
- The passer always becomes the back-up option.
- Players should work off the ball to create space.
- Where space is limited, players must ensure they balance the court.

forward options and a back-up (square option) available for the ball carrier. A player must create the space to receive the ball by working hard off the ball in order to commit and lose the defender.

Shooter Rotation

Rotation in the shooting circle enables the shooters to split the defenders and in turn create options for the ball carrier. The goal shooter and the goal attack must work effectively together, and they must communicate in order to keep the shooting circle balanced at all times. The front shooter takes responsibility and initiates the movement, and the back shooter will be the reactor to ensure that the court area is balanced (width and lengthwise). The front shooter is often the

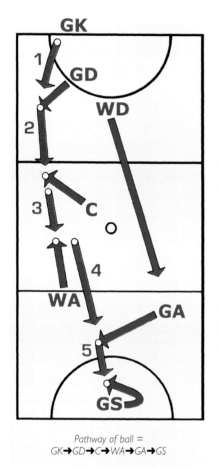

Pathway of ball =
GK➔GD➔C➔WA➔GA➔GS

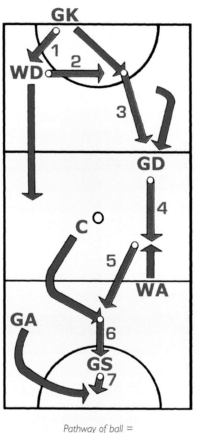

Pathway of ball =
GK➔WD➔GK➔GD➔WA➔C➔GS➔GA

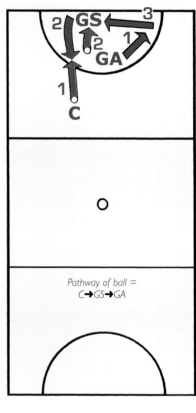

Pathway of ball =
C➔GS➔GA

Shooter rotation.

Two examples of full court systems.

one who will draw the defence and create a passing option to the back shooter. The circle rotation patterns should allow the attacking players to feed a shooter moving towards the post wherever possible.

- The goal attack is the initiator, and leads to their left (see above).
- The reactor (goal shooter) moves to the top of the circle to receive the ball from centre.
- Depending on the location of the goal defence, the goal attack may then be able to receive the ball moving towards the post.

- A more difficult rotation is when the shooters are almost parallel in the circle.
- Here the goal shooter is nearer the ball, hence the initiator, and makes a move forwards towards the ball carrier, but does not receive the ball.
- The goal attack reacts and leads towards the post to receive a pass from the centre.
- Here the goal shooter has opened up the space behind them for the goal attack.

Throughout this chapter the principles of

attack have been applied, and it is vital that attacking players use a variety of movement skills to free themselves from their opponent, such as changes of direction, changes of pace and feint movements. The timing of the move is vital, and without good timing the options available to the ball carrier are reduced. Verbal and non-verbal communication between players is essential to ensure that more than one player does not move for the ball at the same time. Whilst passing options are conveyed in this chapter, the avid reader should seek to locate what other options are present in each of the illustrations.

CHAPTER 11

APPLYING THE PRINCIPLES IN DEFENCE

The Centre Pass

The defending players must communicate effectively to prevent the attacking team executing a fast centre pass using the straight line play. A variety of methods can be employed by the defending players at the centre pass, and it is vital that a team mix up their positioning and change their tactics readily to outwit and counteract the attacking strategies being employed by the opposition. It is the goal defence, wing defence and centre who must work effectively as a unit to place pressure on the centre pass. The defensive unit must operate effectively together during the first and second phase of the centre pass to restrict the options and ultimately turn over the ball before it reaches the goal circle.

DEFENDING STRATEGIES AT THE CENTRE PASS

- Defend in a two-on-one formation.
- Force the goal attack and wing attack wide.
- Zone at the centre pass by goal defence, wing defence and centre.
- Drop back at the centre pass (goal defence, wing defence and centre).
- Keep the attack off the circle edge.

Defending in a Two-on-One Formation

When implementing this tactic at the centre pass the following set-ups can be adopted:
- Wing defence and centre can work as a unit and mark the wing attack.

- Centre and goal defence can mark the goal attack.

Both defenders must work together with good shoulder alignment to close off the gap for the attacking player being marked, and good communication ensures that one of the defenders covers the sprint over the line of this attacker. The non-marker in this instance will pick up the centre player once the pass has been released.

If the goal attack and wing attack are both positioned on the inside of their

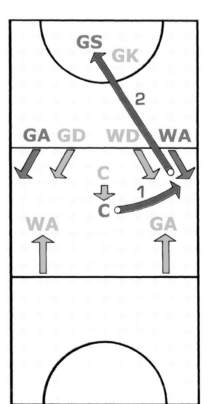

Forcing players wide.

defender, the centre can fill the middle area to quickly mark either player as they move to receive the ball. The illustration below shows this positioning of the three defending players, and the centre must position well forward of the transverse line to be in a good position for the intercept. As the whistle is blown, the goal defence and wing defence must drive out towards the middle channel to close down the available space.

Forcing the Goal Attack and Wing Attack Wide

The defending unit works to force the two attacking players wide at the first phase of the centre pass, which forces the centre to deliver a pass on an angle, which will increase the chance of an error or interception. The wing attack and goal attack on the defending team also move down the court quickly to reduce the space available. The centre player marks the attacking centre one-on-one, forcing a long pass to the shooter, or forcing a back pass. A well executed, third stage defending technique is required here to delay the goal attack and wing attack, and prevent them being involved in subsequent phases of the centre pass. Should the wing attack receive the ball, there is only a long passing option forward to the goal shooter, or a pass back to a supporting player. If the goal keeper is ball side, then the forward option, if given, should be intercepted by this defender.

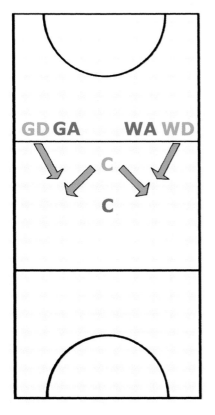

Zoning at the centre pass.

Zoning at the Centre Pass

A zone is where a player marks an area of the court, rather than an opponent. In this case the goal defence, wing defence and centre cover their space, and should the wing attack or goal attack move into their space they will attempt to close off and intercept any pass to them. This strategy ensures that the defending unit fills the middle of the court and restricts the movement of the attacking players. On the whistle, the goal defence and wing defence must jump over the line quickly, and along with the centre who has dropped back, they put a zone on for the first phase of the centre pass. The defending goal attack and wing attack will also move down the court. The defending unit moves over the line and the players cover the spaces, as in illustration (see above).

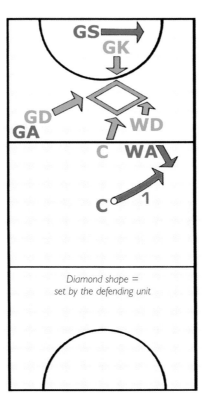

Diamond shape = set by the defending unit

Drop back at the centre pass.

Drop Back at the Centre Pass

The goal defence, wing defence and centre position as if they were going to compete at the first phase of the centre pass. When the whistle is blown the defending unit drops back, and the first pass is therefore delivered easily to one of the attacking players. The defending unit then works together to cover the channel the ball is being passed through. The goal keeper's position creates a diamond shape for this defending unit, and it is the goal keeper who will cover the back space for any possible interception. The nearest defender to the ball carrier will employ stage two defence to mark the ball. The goal defence must assess the strengths of the goal attack and make a well timed decision as to when she should drop to mark the goal attack so as to prevent a shooter entering the circle unmarked.

Keeping the Attack off the Circle Edge

The defending unit must ensure that they position between their opponent and the goal by either marking the ball, dropping back, zoning the immediate space in front of the attacker, or by using the off-line technique. This strategy is particularly effective to prevent a successful pass at the second phase of the centre pass. Should their opponent receive the ball the defender must employ stage two defending, but keep their feet on the ground. If the defender were to execute a jump to intercept at stage two, then the attacker could move forwards after the ball has been released, as the defender would be caught in the air or in the recovery phase of this jump to defend. The defender must track the attacking player and try and force them near the sidelines to restrict the space available and keep them away from the circle edge.

DEFEND AROUND THE EDGE OF THE CIRCLE

- Be ball side.
- Do not give away a penalty through obstruction or contact.
- Do not go offside into the circle.
- Force the wing attack and centre into the corners.
- Attempt the interception and use a strong two-footed take-off from a stationary position.

Goal Line Throw-In

When defending the throw-in, the focus of the defending unit is to restrict space and the available options

In this defending set-up, the wing defence and goal defence can attempt to intercept the pass to the goal attack. The goal defence must also be aware that a pass could be given to the goal shooter. The goal keeper is positioned to go for the high pass to the goal shooter, and also to move to intercept the long pass across the circle to the centre.

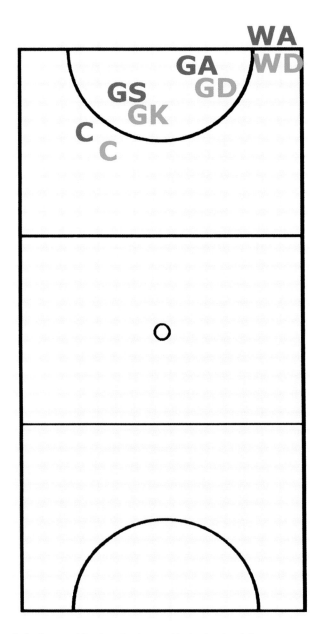

Defending a goal-line throw-in taken outside the shooting circle.

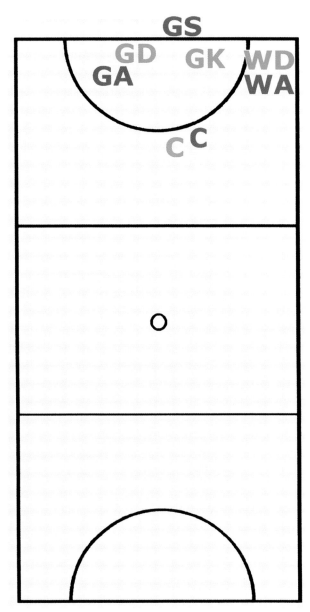

Defending a throw-in taken by the goal shooter.

In the next situation, the centre and wing attack have gained a strong position to receive a pass in the area between them. If the goal keeper feels that an interception at the second stage of defence is not possible, then they should drop back to zone the area in front of the wing attack and centre. The aim here is for the goal keeper not to mark too near the circle so that the ball carrier does not spot the danger of the goal keeper moving for the intercept.

Sideline Throw-In

In both illustrations (opposite page), the defending players must adopt a ball side position and work hard to restrict the options on the straight line of play. All defenders adopt a front defending

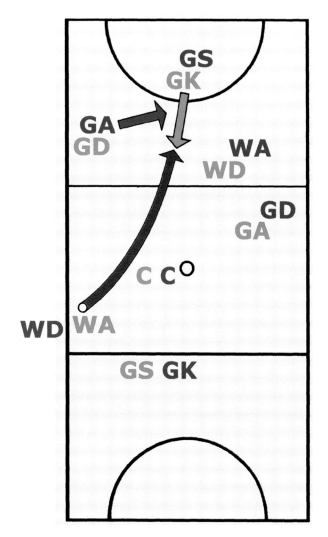

Defending a throw-in from the centre third.

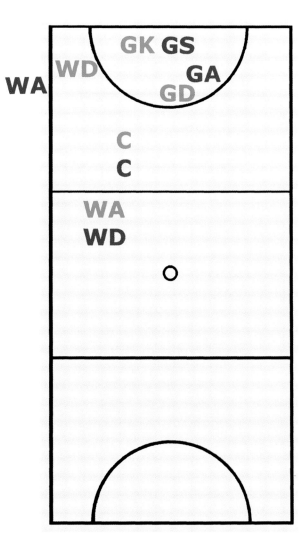

Defending a throw-in from the goal third.

position, and they must be ready to make an interception off their own opponent. All defenders must be trained also to leave their opponent and cover a high ball that may be going to another attacking player in front of them. This is shown above left, where the goal keeper reads the pass to the goal attack, and by timing the move and driving on to the line of the ball, an interception is gained. The goal defence has adopted the front position on the goal attack so requires the support of the goal keeper to cover the back space.

Defending in the Shooting Circle

The goal keeper and goal defence must communicate and work well as a unit to prevent the two shooters accessing the main space for a passing option. The two defenders will adopt a front and back formation, and it is the back defender that must watch the movement and reactions of the front defender. Both defenders will mark in front of their

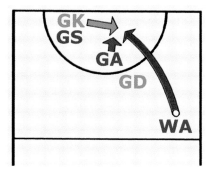

The back defender intercepting.

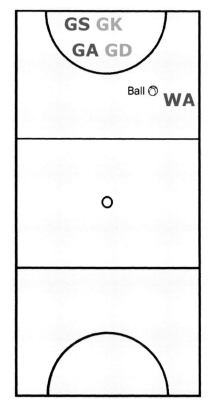

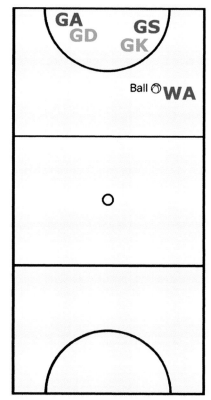

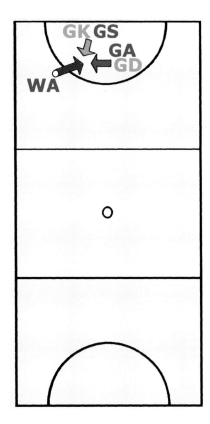

Restricting and denying space by the defenders.

Defence on the front position.

GK takes the intercept.

opponents and keep both the ball and player in view. The back defender must be poised and ready to move off her opponent to intercept the ball being passed to the front shooter.

The two circle defenders must work hard to manoeuvre the goal shooter and goal attack away from the ball, and prevent them accessing the desirable space. The two defenders work and communicate as a unit to position the shooters either on the same side of the circle, or at either side, or to the middle channel.

The two circle defenders must ensure that the shooters do not have space to make a run along the goal line to the post. The goal keeper observes the movement of the goal attack, and similarly the goal defence observes the goal shooter's movement for possible interceptions.

Either defender may call 'switch' if they feel an interchange of opponent will close off options, rather than continuing to track their own opponent.

Zoning

The defence often uses this to outwit and add an element of surprise, and is successful if a team does not have the experience to break the zone through well planned attacking strategies. All individuals setting the zone must have excellent movement skills, good agility, peripheral vision and an ability to intercept. The zone will only be successful if players are aware of the space they are covering, and have the vision to see opponents moving into their space from all angles. The defending unit will often

communicate to team mates in front of themselves to give the best possible chance for an interception.

In the mid-court zone there will be five players (the goal keeper and goal shooter are not allowed in this third, so remain in their working area), each covering their space. The player closest to the ball should call for it, and drive to make the interception whilst the other defenders react and cover the initial space. Good body angles ensure that the ball and all the space can be viewed at any time.

A high zone can also be set up when the opposing team has a goal-line throw-in within their defending third. This involves the goal shooter, goal attack, wing attack and centre filling the space within the goal third to force a passing error or a long-angled pass that can be intercepted.

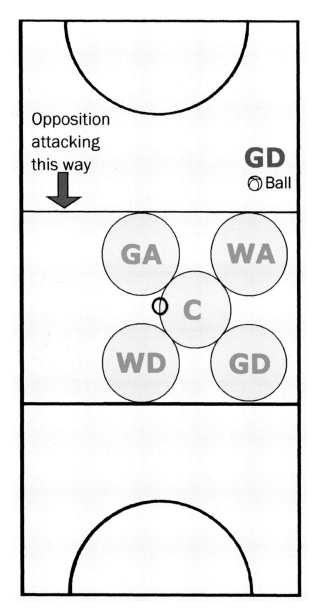

Players positioned in a mid-court zone.

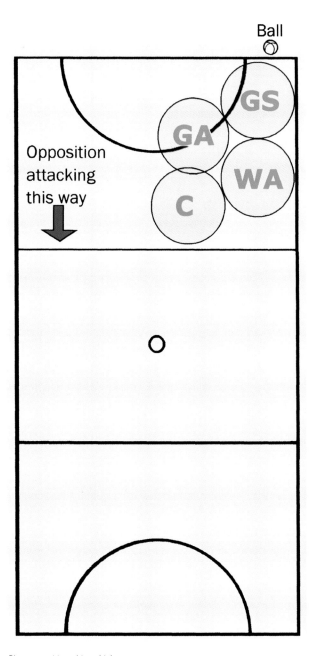

Players positioned in a high-court zone.

Summary

This chapter has highlighted the need for a defender to have a high level of movement and technical skills that can be applied to the defending strategies and tactical plays covered here. Effective communication and team work are essential for any of the above strategies to be effective. A defending team must be able to make fast and accurate decisions to ensure that the most effective defending strategies are employed to provide the best possible opportunities for a turnover.

PART 4

TRAINING

CHAPTER 12

THE PRINCIPLES OF TRAINING

Any training programmes are devised in accordance with the training principles that have been well documented across sports. Training programmes and sessions must adhere to these principles to ensure that demands are being placed on the correct energy system. In applying these principles of training the performer will ensure that physiological adaptations are made.

TRAINING PRINCIPLES

- Individuality
- Adaptation
- Overload
- Progression
- Specificity
- Variation
- Reversibility
- Recovery

Individuality

Training programmes must meet the needs of individuals, as each person will respond to training differently. The principles of long-term athlete development should be addressed, and consideration should be given to the development and training ages of the performer. There is evidence to suggest that many netball players will participate in identical training programmes, and it is vital that each player is attended to, and allocated an individualized programme.

Adaptation

A successful training programme will result in physical improvement, but it is important to note that changes may take place over the training period and the immediate effect may not be visible. For adaptations to occur, the body systems must be repeatedly placed under stress.

The Overcompensation Model

During a training session the performer will encounter fatigue if they continue for a long period of time, and if they continued to perform the training task, there would be a decrease in the intensity. It is in the recovery period that

A performance gym for training.

the adaptations to the training load take place, and this is referred to as 'overcompensation'. Therefore the recovery time after training is critical, and after this period of rest the body will be able to train at a higher level. This process of overcompensation governs all types of training, whether it is physical, tactical, technical or psychological.

Overload

In order to gain an adaptation effect, the training load must place the body under increased stress. The intensity of this stress must be greater than that usually required in a match situation, and out of the comfort zone of the performer. Individualizing the training load for each performer is essential, because if the load is too high, injury and pain could result, and if too low there will be no improvement.

Achieving the correct training load is a result of managing the volume and intensity of any training, and when planning a training session or programme the FITT principles indicated in the box below must be adhered to.

ACHIEVING THE CORRECT TRAINING LOAD

- **Frequency:** How often will the training sessions occur?
- **Intensity:** How hard should the player train, and how close to their maximum level?
- **Time:** How long should the performer work (for example the number of sets or repetitions)?
- **Type:** What is the focus of the training (for example endurance, speed, strength)?

Progression

For performance improvements to continue, the training programme must increase in complexity and demand. It is

therefore vital that an increase in training load occurs at the right time and at the right level for the performer. For example, in strength training programmes there would be an increase in weight to be lifted, or in an endurance session the rest period would be reduced. A coach must therefore integrate all aspects of performance into a training plan by dividing up the training year into a set of training phases that are progressive in terms of purpose, volume and intensity. This phasing is known as 'periodization', and ensures that progressive steps and action plans are in place to improve performance in the short and longer term.

Specificity

Adaptation will occur in relation to the activity being performed in training. Any training programme in netball must relate to the demands of the game and should consider the specific netball movements, the muscle groups utilized, the length of the work period, and the work-to-rest ratios. A coach must therefore identify the fitness component that underpins a particular performance component, and devise an accurate training programme. For example, a player wants to improve their speed when sprinting out at a centre pass, so must therefore work at a high intensity and for a short duration. The performer should work for no more than 10sec on this task, and there must be 20sec recovery time.

Variation

Any coach must offer a variety of activities within a training programme so that tedium is prevented. The constant repetition of a practice or training task reduces motivation, and the coach must address the practice schedules to ensure that a variety of training tasks are implemented. A good coach will try and introduce a novel task in every session to ensure that the group remains motivated.

Reversibility

'If you don't use it, you lose it' is a phrase often associated with reversibility. By reducing the training load or becoming inactive, the level of adaptation will be reduced. All performers must therefore train regularly, and when a fitness component is not a priority in a training phase they must still follow a maintenance programme. Scientific studies have found that three weeks of bed rest as a result of illness can result in a reduction of aerobic endurance by 25 per cent. A coach must therefore ensure that a performer is able to recover from the demands of their sport in the off season, but also maintain their fitness in this transition period.

Recovery

Rest is often termed as one of the most important principles, and without sufficient rest or recovery periods, physical adaptations cannot occur. Rest and recovery time are just as important within a training session, and should be set based upon the volume and intensity of exercise being undertaken. Within the training schedule an intense training session should result in subsequent sessions of a lower intensity, or total rest. Coaches should carefully integrate and manipulate training loads by alternating the heavy, medium and light sessions during a weekly cycle. If a performer trains once per day and follows a programme of varying training loads in each session, it is often possible to recover completely in twenty-four hours.

In Summary

The effective coach will ensure that all training programmes devised apply these training principles to ensure that a suitable training load is administered for the performer. Alongside this carefully planned and integrated scientific programme the coach must communicate effectively with the performer to devise, monitor and evaluate aspects of the training programme.

CHAPTER 13

ENERGY SYSTEMS AND PHYSIOLOGICAL DEMANDS IN NETBALL

Success in netball requires a player to be trained in all the components of fitness (endurance, speed, strength, power, agility and flexibility), and coaches must ensure that players exercise at intensities that equate to those experienced in match conditions. A coach must ensure the training programme is designed according to scientific training principles in order to improve a player's on-court performance.

During a match there could be a total of 170 goals attempted, with converted goals resulting in a 5sec delay before play restarts at the centre pass – which is why netball is often described as an interval game requiring both aerobic and anaerobic energy sources. Players will often execute several short sprints, interspersed with short recovery periods throughout the duration of a game.

Players need a high level of skill, aerobic and anaerobic fitness, and the body uses three energy systems that work simultaneously. The contribution of each system depends upon the intensity and duration of the physical activity. The ATP-PC and the lactic acid system operate without the use of oxygen.

The ATP-PC system provides an immediate source of energy for high intensity activities such as jumping, short sprints and throwing. This system can only provide energy for 10sec, and the body requires approximately 20sec recovery time before the intensity can be repeated.

The lactic acid system provides an energy supply for high intensity work ranging from 2–3min. This system does not require oxygen, as it utilizes glucose as the source of energy. Lactic acid is a by-product of this system, and this can cause muscular cramps and discomfort; as fatigue sets in, there is a rapid decrease in performance. A player would need 2–3min to recover before the equivalent intensity of work could be carried out again.

The aerobic energy system provides a steady supply of energy throughout the duration of a game, and a player must have a trained cardiovascular system in order to provide the necessary amounts of oxygen. A coach must understand the contribution of the three energy systems when planning training programmes to ensure that players maintain appropriate work-to-rest ratios within a training session. The intensities experienced in training should simulate those encountered in a competitive match.

Most netball players train together and complete identical training tasks, which can mean that the physiological demands of the seven playing positions are often disregarded. In terms of acceleration, the sprinting efforts of players lasts for 2sec, and there are approximately 100 of these executed by a player in any one game. A study carried out by Allison (1978) identified that there are significant differences in the amount of time spent sprinting between the playing positions (see box below).

TIME SPRINTING IN A GAME (%)

Wing attack/wing defence	16.3%
Centre	11.8%
Goal attack/goal defence	5.9%
Goal shooter/goal keeper	4.1%

Recordings of player movements indicate the following differences between the playing positions:

- The defensive players shuffled more.
- The centre spent the highest amount of time slow jogging.
- The centre has the least amount of rest time.
- Centres executed more passes than any other position.
- Jumping actions were executed the most by circle players.

By comparing four of the playing positions – centre, goal shooter, goal keeper and goal defence – the following information provides useful guidance for devising training schedules: the goal shooter caught the ball on more occasions than the other positions, and was stationary for a considerable amount of time during the game. It is also important to note that the goal shooter in this analysis had the lowest heart rate throughout the match. The goal shooter spent less time jogging when compared to the centre and goal defence position, but did execute similar locomotor activities when compared to the goal keeper (for example, shuffling).

The centre position was involved in far more sprinting and jogging throughout the game when compared to the other positions, highlighting the dominance of running at a steady state interspersed with sudden sprinting movements. A centre will run an average of 6km per game at the élite level. The goal keeper and goal defence were involved in more jumping and shuffling movements than any other position reviewed. The goal keeper had similar movement patterns to the goal shooter, and often a jump was executed from a stationary position, unlike the jumps executed on the move by the other court positions.

CHAPTER 14

THE FITNESS MONITORING PROTOCOL FOR NETBALL

Fitness monitoring provides the coach with specific information about an individual's performance, and provides the coach with baseline information for designing a training programme. England Netball recommends field-based tests as opposed to laboratory testing, as they are more accessible and cost effective. Field-based tests are selected to reflect the demands of the sport, and they provide relevant performance measurements. The field-based tests used in netball provide a coach with information on the strengths and weaknesses of individual players, and are used to monitor progress throughout the programme. Testing is also a useful mechanism for assessing the effectiveness of a particular training schedule, and a coach would use such information to modify the programme if the training were not having the desired effect.

The battery of fitness tests should not always be carried out within the same mesocycle: for example, if players are working on speed, then the appropriate speed test to assess an individual's level and progress should be selected. For players, the tests often serve as a motivational tool, and provide the individual with a self-referenced measure of progress. Fitness monitoring should not be used to compare the fitness levels of a group of players, or be used as the single criterion for selection or de-selection purposes. An effective training programme will have testing every eight to ten weeks. A coach should schedule the testing and inform players, rather than impose on them without warning. Monitoring is often carried out at the following times: prior to the preparation phase in order to obtain baseline measures; and at the end of the competition phase, to check whether the intensity of training has been appropriate to maintain fitness in this phase.

It is vital that any individual being tested does not participate in any physical activity in the twenty-four hours prior to the testing. A coach should make attempts always to test the players at the same time of day, and to ensure consistency in the conditions (for example the facility used, the cleanliness of the floor, temperature of the hall, the same warm-up, the same ordering of tests). The tests should always be standardized, and the coach should adhere to the documented procedure and guidelines.

Testing Protocols for Netball

England Netball has developed a number of field-based tests that are appropriate for players at different levels. All players should have their height and weight

measurements taken, and on occasions skin-fold measurements are utilized to provide information on body structure.

2

The vertical jump test.

Potential Players

For individuals who attend regional 'potential' training camps, the following three tests are administered.

The Throwing Test

This test is a measure of the muscular endurance of the arms and chest, and indicates for how long an individual may be able to keep throwing a hard pass during a game of netball. For this test an individual must stand behind a line drawn 3m away from a wall, and throw a netball against the wall and catch it as many times as they can in one minute.

Vertical Jump Test

This is a test of leg strength and power, and indicates how high a player may jump to catch or intercept a ball in the game. They must stand sideways on to the wall with hands on hips, and crouch down and immediately jump as high as they can. The nearest hand should hit the wall so that the difference in height between the jump height and the standing reach height may be calculated.

Multi-Stage Fitness Test (MSFT)

This is a shuttle-run test, and offers an accurate measure of an individual's cardiovascular fitness. They must run continuously back and forth between two markers 20m apart, keeping up and in time with a series of bleeps on a CD. The test commences at a low intensity, and gradually increases by decreasing the amount of time to get from one marker to the other. When a player can no longer keep up with the bleeps and misses the line on three consecutive shuttles, they must withdraw from the test.

TARGET SCORES FOR POTENTIAL PLAYERS	
Throwing test	50
Vertical jump	28cm
MSFT	10.1

Talent Squad Athletes

Individuals who are placed within a talent squad ('training to train phase') will complete the following tests in addition to the vertical jump and MSFT outlined above.

Medicine Ball Throw

Arm and shoulder strength is measured by using a medicine ball to execute a chest pass. An individual sits with their back pressed against the wall to restrict the movement of the back, with the feet in front and a hip-width apart (there must be a 90-degree angle at the hip joint). They hold the medicine ball at chest height close to the body, and throw it as far as possible. The distance thrown is measured from the base of the wall, and not from the individual's feet. The best of three trials is recorded for each test, and a 4kg (9lb) medicine ball is used.

505 Agility Sprint

This test involves a single change of direction and measures the individual's ability to decelerate, change direction, and accelerate from changes of direction.

The first of the eight tasks: squats.

A timing gate is used to record the time taken, with the test being performed using the left and right foot for the change of direction. The individual must sprint through the timing gate to the pivot line, change direction with one foot, and accelerate out of the pivot before sprinting back through the timing gate. They have three trials, with the best fastest score being recorded to $\frac{1}{100}$sec.

10m Sprint

This test requires the individual to sprint over a distance of 10m from a standing start. Electronic timing gates are used to record the time, and the best of three trials is recorded.

TARGET SCORES FOR TALENT SQUAD ATHLETES	
Medicine ball throw	3.5–3.8m
Vertical jump	32–36cm
MSFT	10.5–11.1
505	2.45sec
10m sprint	<1.9sec

Open Squad Athletes

More detailed testing is carried out with the England Open Squad, and the following tests are administered at this élite level: MSFT, 505 agility, vertical jump,

5m, 10m and 20m sprints (protocol as per the 10m sprint outlined above), and functional mobility assessments.

Functional Mobility

TARGET SCORES FOR OPEN SQUAD ATHLETES		
Test	Acceptable	Desirable
Vertical jump	40	45cm
MSFT	11.7	12.1
505	2.35	2.30sec
5m sprint	1.15	1.10sec
10m sprint	1.95	1.90sec
20m sprint	3.25	3.20sec

Hurdle step.

Scapula humeral rhythm (abduction/adduction).

Rotation strength and stability – Swiss ball Russian twist.

Trunk stability – push-up.

Split squat.

Active straight leg raise.

This assessment is designed to provide a measure of an athlete's movement capability, and to identify any muscular imbalance or weak areas. The eight assessment tests have been selected to represent the movement patterns executed in the game of netball, and are outlined in the illustrations in this chapter.

1 Squats
2 Hurdle step
3 Scapula humeral rhythm (abduction/adduction)
4 Rotation strength and stability – Swiss ball Russian twist
5 Trunk stability – push-up
6 Split squat
7 Active straight leg raise
8 Dynamic single leg stability

Coaches can use the norm tables to provide feedback to the individuals, and the results should be fed back in a positive and constructive manner. Individuals who have a low training age may score much lower than those who have engaged with more serious training, so it is vital that subsequent tests are carried out to see improvements.

Dynamic single leg stability.

CHAPTER 15

PERIODIZATION AND THE TRAINING PLAN

Coaches must carefully balance the components of training (volume and intensity) in order to promote optimal training adaptation and thus prevent overtraining. Training programmes must be divided into separate training periods, with each encompassing different goals and training methods. Each period is designed to maximize the gains in the various components of performance, and will contain training loads that are calculated with appropriate regeneration/recovery periods.

To achieve this systematic, progressive and integrated training programme, the principles governing the process of periodization must be applied. Periodization will ensure that an individual's training is coordinated to allow them to achieve a peak in performance for the key competitions. Overall, periodization applies the principle of overload – recovery – peaking so as to maximize performance.

KEY POINTS

A successful coach will:
- Plan systematically to ensure organized training and preparation.
- Consider the work and study commitments of each athlete.
- Consider performances in the fitness tests and previous competition.
- Integrate all the performance factors into the training programme.
- Divide the training year into a group of fluid and overlapping training periods.
- Relate the training periods to the individual's needs, stage of development, and timing of the key competitions.
- Prioritize competitions, and ensure that peaking occurs for the major competition(s).

Structure of the Training Plan

The training plan is broken down into phases referred to as macro-, meso- and microcycles. The cycles represent three layers of training period, all inter-related to form the progressive and individualized training programme.

Macrocycle

This is a long-term training phase; in netball it is often represented as the full season, and would lead a performer into a major annual competition. England Netball as a governing body has recently reviewed the competition structure to prevent the need for multiple peaks in performance by reducing the duration of the competitive cycle; at the most, individuals would only be expected to train for a double peak in performance. Thus, should an England Open squad be training for a major championship such as the Commonwealth Games or World Netball Championships, then the top domestic competition would be aligned and integrated to ensure it supported the periodized plan.

A competitive season demanding multiple peaking for competitions is detrimental to the long-term development of any athlete, and England Netball now boasts a competitive programme whereby individuals perform in the correct tier of competition and maintain suitable training-to-competition ratios.

All macrocycles contain three main training phases: preparation, competition and transition (recovery period).

The Preparation Phase

During this initial phase the individual will prepare for the demands of the competition phase. This phase is further divided into the 'general preparation period' (GPP) and the 'specific preparation period' (SPP). In the GPP, the focus is on general physical conditioning, and this is also where the foundations are established in all components of performance. The player will work at a low intensity in training, but will complete several sessions (high volume). A coach should complete a review of the previous season, and from this, identify the needs of the performer in terms of the technical and tactical work to be addressed in this phase. For example, a player may be required to break down and master a particular passing technique or method of getting free.

The player will progress into the SPP where more sport-specific training is carried out at a greater intensity. This phase represents the transition from general conditioning to more competition-specific training where the technical and tactical skills are worked on. The SPP is shorter than the GPP, and throughout the preparation period the volume of training will progressively decrease as its intensity increases. Here the performer will practise their technical and tactical skills under an increased amount of pressure, and begin to develop their tactical understanding. A coach must ensure that game plans are practised and refined in this phase – for example, defending the centre pass to goal.

For an athlete competing in the Netball Super League (NSL) competition, the preparation phase would normally take place ten to twelve weeks before the season commences (for example, week 1 in August to mid-October).

Competition Phase

The main objective in this phase is to gradually develop peak performance, and the training completed here is court-specific and anaerobic in nature. As the main competition period approaches, there is a need to taper the training in order to peak for the main competition. Here the training volume decreases, and a coach will engage the performer in simulation activities that replicate the competition conditions. As the competition phase progresses, the emphasis is on more netball-specific training, and there should be an emphasis on improving speed and sprint recovery and leg power and agility.

The coach in this phase should ensure that the focus is on the strengths of a performer and the team, as opposed to reviewing the areas requiring development. In terms of the technical and tactical aspects of performance, it is vital in this phase that the players fine tune their match strategies in relation to their opposition's strengths and weaknesses.

The competition phase is normally between mid-October to mid-April for an athlete competing in the NSL competition.

Transition or Recovery Phase

This phase occurs at the end of the competition period and is a period of active rest. The main focus of this phase is recovery and recuperation following a demanding competition phase.

KEY POINTS

Training emphasis (% of time allocated to each component):

	GPP	SPP	Competition
Conditioning	50%	25%	10%
Technical	30%	25%	10%
Tactical	10%	25%	40%
Psychological	10%	25%	40%

The individual is given the opportunity to recover both mentally and physically from the demands of the competition schedule. Active rest is recommended, where the individual will take part in low-intensity activity (such as swimming and cycling) to prevent a complete loss of fitness. The length of this phase is dependent upon the duration of the competition phase.

Mesocycle

Mesocycles are subdivisions of the macrocycles, and often span a period of two to six weeks. Several mesocycles make up a training phase, each having their own specified objectives, which ensures a progressive programme of training.

An Example of a Mesocycle

Phase: Specific preparation period (mesocycle 2a)
Duration: 3 weeks
Sessions per week: 4 (taper in week 3 for adaptation)
Work-to-rest ratio: 1:4
Fitness priorities: *Anaerobic:* short court interval sprints (45–70sec); *Strength:* Hypertrophy and general strength; *Speed/agility:* short acceleration/reaction to stimulus

Microcycle

This is a training period, and in most sports spans a seven-day period. It outlines in detail to the performer the information regarding specific training activities, intensity and volume.

CHAPTER 16

PLANNING THE NETBALL SESSION

A successful coaching session is planned, and relates closely to the overall annual plan. It goes without saying that those coaches who fail to plan will undoubtedly plan to fail. The coach must always adopt a player-centred approach, and doing this will ensure that the needs of the players are put first, rather than the activity, parents, coach goals and ambitions. Each individual – whatever their age, ability or disability – in a session must be viewed as an

---

THE CONTENT OF A SESSION

- Introduction and warm-up.
- Skill development section.
- A competitive element (a small side or full game).
- A cool-down and conclusion.

---

individual with unique needs, interests and goals. A coach who possesses the knowledge of how a session should be structured will be able to deliver a session that contains appropriate progression, and ultimately achieves its purpose.

The session plan outline assists the coach in structuring and designing a session, and it is recommended that all coaches complete one of these for each session delivered.

Date		Venue		Duration		Number		Equipment	
Session Goals						Personal Coaching Goals			

Content	Time	Task and Group Management	Coaching Points
Introduction/warm-up			
Skill development/practices			
Game/modified game Conditioned FOCUS:			

The session plan pro-forma.

A Step-by-Step Guide to Session Planning

Session Goals

It is essential that the coach states clearly what the players should be able to do by the end of a session, and the intentions are stated as session goals on the plan. There should not be too many goals to achieve, and the goals must be measurable – for example, to be able to execute a shoulder pass at the appropriate time.

A coach should use the SMART acronym to ensure that the goals set are accurate. Thus all goals should be:

Specific: For example, use a change of direction to get free at the appropriate time.
Measurable: For example, always look to pass forwards for the first option.
Adjustable: Through monitoring of progress the goal may not be achievable, allowing the coach to make necessary adjustments.
Realistic: A goal should be challenging but within reach for a performer.
Time-based: Goals should be set for the session (short term), and they should link closely to the intermediate and long-term goals for the players.

A coach should also set personal goals for the session, which relate to their own coaching skills and performance. The personal goals allow a coach to continue in their professional development by continually reviewing their performances.

Equipment

A coach should know what equipment is available in order to plan for the session, and this should be appropriate for the group; for example, Under 11 players will use size 4 netballs as opposed to size 5.

Duration

It is vital in the planning stages that the coach is aware of the duration of the session. The length of a session should take account of the playing level and stage of development of the individuals: for example, a 90min session should be the maximum time for a potential player, whereas an open age group player will often train for a two-hour period. In the planning stage a coach should ensure that the time is maximized by planning smooth transitions from one activity to another. Once the content of the session has been decided, the coach should allocate a period of time to each phase of the session, acknowledging the transition time between activities.

Number of Players

A coach should know how many players will be at the session, and should also give consideration to the different ability levels, development and training ages. Any individual medical or health issues should also be considered in the light of the content.

Content

There are several factors that could impact upon the content of a session: for example, the stage in the season, previous performances in competition and training,

---

PROGRESSIONS FOR PASSING PRACTICES

- Static players.
- Players on the move.
- Increase the number of players for passing options.
- Add direction to the practice (moving to goal).
- Reduce the space available.
- Add defenders (passive – active).
- Set play situations (centre pass, sideline throw-in).
- Small side game.

---

lifestyle issues and player motivation. A coach should select the practices, progressions and game activities required to achieve the session goals. Progressions should be carefully planned to ensure an appropriate increase in complexity. All progressions should begin in a closed practice situation – no defenders, limited movement and a small number of players – and gradually increase in terms of complexity, pressure situations and the level of decision making expected from the players in the practice.

It is also important to be able to adapt any practice planned should the number of participants change: for example, planning for an even number, and one player does not attend the session. Some players may find a practice too easy or too difficult than others, and so alternative tasks or targets will need to be planned should this happen.

For each practice, the coach should ensure that one or two coaching points are stated on the session plan to ensure that the participants have clear points to focus on in order to improve their performance.

Adapting an Activity

Activities will need to be adapted to suit all individuals within a session, as there may be individual differences related to ability, experience, developmental level, physiological aspects and attention span. Tips for adapting an activity include the following:

- Modify the equipment – such as lowering the post, using a smaller ball.
- Adapt the rules – stipulate no overhead pass to ensure that certain skills are practised, or that shooters can only shoot from the inner area of the circle.
- Modify the practice by making the area smaller if the practice focus is on getting free from an opponent, or increase the area if the practice has a defending focus. Increasing the number of players in a practice means a ball carrier has more decisions to make.
- Individuals with special needs must not be neglected, and players with visual impairments will require a coach to use their name more frequently; also, using a

ball with a bell inside is a useful aid. Individuals with speech or hearing impairments will need more time to convey their thoughts, and the coach should use visual cues where possible: for example, the umpire may have a flag to raise if the whistle cannot be heard when an infringement has occurred.

Volume and Intensity

A coach must ensure that there are a sufficient number of hydration breaks within the session, and also that participants have appropriate work-to-rest ratios. If a practice involves sprinting – for example, sprinting to receive a pass over 10m – a player must ensure that the appropriate work rate is maintained, otherwise the practice effect cannot be achieved. When working on a practice involving short sprints, an individual on average will be able to complete between six and eight repetitions before performance levels deteriorate. This period of work should be followed by a rest period, giving time for the body to recover (work-to-rest = 1:2, or 1:3 depending on fitness levels).

Task and Group Management

When planning the session a coach must ensure that all space is used effectively, and that groups have clear boundaries within which they will practise. The session plan should identify the areas within which the groups will work, and often a coach will use the court markings or cones to communicate the working areas to the group. The illustration to the left shows how a court can be divided for effective use of space when practising

Grouping is also a key consideration when planning, and a coach can group according to ability, friendship, developmental level, or randomly. Ensuring that individuals are challenged in the group activities is a paramount concern, and so ability groupings may be more beneficial. A coach should vary the groupings within and between sessions to ensure that individuals are able to work with a range of players as the season progresses.

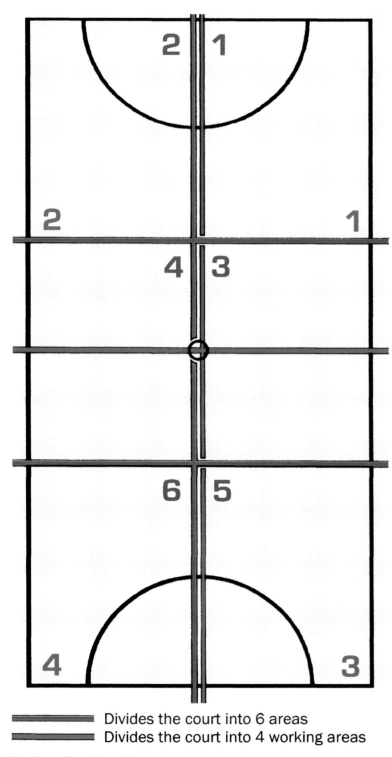

Divides the court into 6 areas
Divides the court into 4 working areas

Dividing the court for training sessions.

The Warm-Up

The warm-up should prepare players mentally and physically for the subsequent activities by incorporating dynamic mobility activities and ball work.

Dynamic Movement Skills for a Warm-Up

The following dynamic movement activities are examples of what should feature in the early stages of the warm-up, and once completed, the netball-specific ball work can begin. Examples include the following:

- Sidestepping, leading with the right and left leg.
- Skipping with a low knee lift.
- Skipping with a high knee lift, adding arm swings.
- Stretch the calf muscle in the lunge position, and simultaneously swing one arm in a spiral pattern, repeating on the other leg.
- Carioca stepping, followed by wide leg squats (lead left, then right leg).
- Lungeing forwards in a variety of

TOP TIPS FOR THE WARM-UP

- Start slowly and gradually increase the intensity.
- Activities should be relevant to the focus of the skill section.
- Include dynamic mobility, not static stretching.
- Vary the activities and make them fun.

---

directions, and simultaneously reaching arms into various directions.

- Ankle rolls for 10m, heel flicks for 10m, ankle rolls, followed by a two-footed jump.
- Falling start, then sprint forwards with three quick steps, and repeat.
- Hamstring stretch in a standing position whilst turning the trunk to either side. Repeat with the other leg.
- Sprint forwards for five strides, stop, return backwards with diagonal stepovers to the right. Repeat, but then diagonally back to the left. Repeat to complete three in each direction.

The Cool-Down

This component of the session comes at the end, and allows time for players to carry out exercises to assist the body in returning to its normal resting level in terms of heart rate, blood pressure, adrenalin levels and temperature. The cool-down will rid the body of waste material (lactic acid), as the legs will have a build-up of this waste following a training session or game. Players should gradually reduce the intensity of the exercise in this phase, and move from an upright position to a position of rest on the floor, with the legs elevated to remove waste products.

The cool-down should encompass five to ten minutes of aerobic exercise, and stretching exercises that work on improving flexibility, and a player must refuel and re-hydrate in this phase.

Coaching Style

In the final stage of preparing the session plan, a coach must identify the most appropriate coaching style for each activity. Often a coach will need to introduce new skills or tactics, and will need to adopt a 'tell and show' approach; however, if a task includes decision making, the coach may wish to use a questioning style to encourage self-analysis and reflection. A coach may also wish to set up a practice, and stand back to observe, allowing players to take greater responsibility for learning and the correction of errors.

The coach is involved in a cyclical coaching process whereby he or she will plan, deliver and review a coaching session. All stages are important and should be valued equally by all coaches to ensure success.

TOP TIPS FOR PLANNING

- Ensure progression from one session to the next.
- All practices should be appropriate for the level of participant.
- Safety aspects should have been considered.
- Allow sufficient time on task for participants to practise.
- Reduce transition time between activities.
- Vary the practices and activities.
- Session content should relate to the session goal(s).

CHAPTER 17

PHYSIOLOGICAL FITNESS

A strength and conditioning programme is an essential feature of any performance programme, and the following guidelines must be addressed when scheduling any training:

- A warm-up and cool-down must be incorporated into the fitness session.
- Training days should be interspersed with rest.
- Do not complete an endurance session on more than two consecutive days.
- There should be forty-eight hours between strength sessions.
- If more than one training session is scheduled on a particular day, allow three hours in between and have a light meal between the sessions.
- There should be at least one recovery day per week.
- Sessions should be completed at the correct intensity.

Intensity

The training session intensity is often stated in terms of a percentage of an individual's maximum heart rate (MHR). A simple method to calculate the MHR is to subtract your age from 220: for example, a sixteen-year-old would have an MHR of 204 (220–16). The England Netball talent programme recommends that the following procedure be followed to calculate the MHR:

- Warm up.
- Perform one 800m run at maximum intensity/effort.
- Rest for 60sec.
- Repeat the 800m, and sprint the last 20–30sec.
- Measure your heart rate (wrist or neck) over 15sec and multiply it by four.
- This will represent the MHR (e.g. fifty-one beats in 15sec = 204)

KEY FACTS

Training levels for an individual with an MHR of 204:

- 55–60% of MHR = 112–133 beats per minute (bpm)
- 66–75% of MHR = 135–153 bpm
- 76–80% of MHR = 155–163 bpm
- 81–90% of MHR = 165–184 bpm
- >91% of MHR = 186 bpm

Aerobic Conditioning Programmes

Aerobic conditioning training will ensure that an individual is able to sustain a high work rate throughout a game, and also enables them to recover more quickly from periods of high intensity work during a game. This type of training often occurs in the pre-season phase, but a player must ensure that this aerobic base is maintained throughout the competition phase. The following is an example of a pre-season aerobic conditioning programme suitable for any individual in the pre-season phase of training.

In the pre-season phase it is essential that a good aerobic base is maintained and developed. In order to develop endurance the appropriate activities should be performed three to four times per week for approximately 30min. Netball requires a high level of aerobic endurance for two reasons: first, to ensure that energy can be produced for the duration of the game; and second, to recover quickly from sudden, sharp and intense bursts of concentrated anaerobic activity such as sprinting. Developing a sound aerobic endurance base in the pre-season will

result in greater efficiency in terms of recovery, concentration levels and skill execution in the competition phase.

The training will be of a low intensity but higher in volume, and individuals should work between 70–75 per cent of the maximum working heart rate (MWHR) for the adaptations to occur. Some of the activities that can improve aerobic endurance are aerobics, swimming, running and cycling; tennis, basketball and squash will also provide aerobic training, and these sports also require similar movements to netball.

Varying the sessions within a particular week tends to improve adherence, increase motivation and reduce the risk of injury. An example of a pre-season endurance programme is outlined below:

The Netball DIY Triathlon

(Monday: swim, Wednesday: cycle, Friday: run) – See box for Six-Week Programme.

The England Netball potential talent training programme advocates three endurance training activities, court interval sessions, running interval sessions and steady running sessions. There should be three endurance sessions in any full training week (twenty-six weeks of high intensity training within the annual programme), and two sessions in an unloading week (twenty weeks of a moderate intensity training load, which is between 50 and 75 per cent of a full week). The other six weeks in the year are rest weeks, with no scheduled training.

The table overleaf highlights the number of each training activity to be completed within the phases of the training programme; where the individual is in an unloading week, only two of the sessions should be selected for completion.

PHASE		SESSION 1	SESSION 2	SESSION 3
Phase 1	Weeks 1–13	Court intervals	Running intervals	Steady running
Phase 2	Weeks 14–26	Court intervals	Running intervals	Steady running
Phase 3	Weeks 27–39	Court intervals	Running intervals	Running intervals
Phase 4	Weeks 40–52	Court intervals	Court intervals	Running intervals

SIX-WEEK PROGRAMME

- 100m warm-up should be carried out for all programmes – cool-down should be 100m of side-stroke or breaststroke.

	Distance	Time per length	Recovery
Swim	a) 25m × 6	30sec REST	30sec
Week 1–2	b) 50m × 4	1 min REST	1min
	c) 100m × 2	2min	2 min
Weeks 3–4	As above, but reduce recovery time by 5sec in b) & c).		
Weeks 5–6	As weeks 1–2, but reduce recovery time in a) by 5sec, and in b) & c) by 10sec.		

- Rest for 2–3min between sets (reduce by 10sec per week).
- Recovery time may need adjusting according to fitness.
- Prescribed for a player reaching level 9.5 on the multi-stage fitness test.
- 100m warm-up should be carried out for all programmes – cool-down should be 100m of side-stroke or breaststroke.

Cycle
Weeks 1, 3 & 5	Continuous 20min; try and increase by 1min each week. 70–75% maximum working heart rate (MWHR).
Weeks 2, 4 & 6	18min Fartlek 4min slow + 2min fast (MWHR 75%) – repeat × 3; try and decrease slow cycle by 30sec–1min each week.

Run
Week 1	20min continuous run (70–75% MWHR). Or 4 × 5min (walking for 1.5min and running for 3.5min).
Week 2	22min continuous run. Or 2min jog followed by 4 × 5min (walking for 1.5min and running for 3.5min).
Weeks 3 & 4	24min continuous run. Or 4 × 6min (1.5min walk and 4.5min run combinations).
Weeks 5 & 6	30min continuous run. Or 5 × 6min (1.5min walk and 4.5min run combinations).

- The time spent walking and running will vary according to fitness.
- The time spent running should increase by 30sec to 1min each week.

Court Interval Sessions

The training programme highlights four phases, and there is a clear progression in terms of the workload in relation to repetitions (reps) – for example, the number of times to complete the drill in a set; sets – for example, the number of consecutive repetitions followed by a period of rest; work period – for example, the length of time allowed to complete the drill; and recovery – for example, the

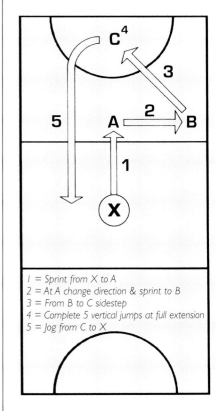

1 = Sprint from X to A
2 = At A change direction & sprint to B
3 = From B to C sidestep
4 = Complete 5 vertical jumps at full extension
5 = Jog from C to X

Examples of court interval sessions.

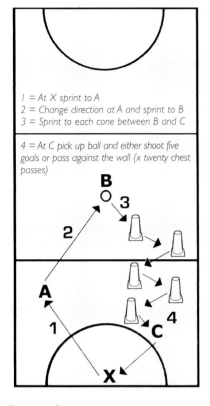

1 = At X sprint to A
2 = Change direction at A and sprint to B
3 = Sprint to each cone between B and C

4 = At C pick up ball and either shoot five goals or pass against the wall (x twenty chest passes)

Examples of court interval sessions.

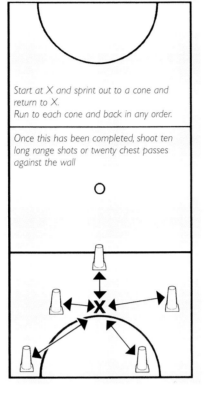

Start at X and sprint out to a cone and return to X.
Run to each cone and back in any order.

Once this has been completed, shoot ten long range shots or twenty chest passes against the wall

Examples of court interval sessions.

length of time to recover between sets and the percentage of the maximum heart rate.

Running Interval Sessions

For any potential athlete the running intervals should be completed at the highest possible work rate for the period of time indicated. Once again, the phases of the programme indicate progression throughout the training period.

Steady Running Sessions

Once again, the England Netball potential training programme states that these sessions must be carried out at the highest even pace an individual can sustain for the work period.

STEADY RUNNING SESSION GUIDELINES		
	Session 1	Session 2
Phase 1	30–45min	30–45min
Phase 2	30–45min	30–45min
Phase 3	45min	–
Phase 4	45min	–

Strength Training Programmes

England Netball recommends that a potential athlete should complete two strength sessions in any full training week, and one session in an unloading week. It is vital the correct tempo is maintained when completing the exercise: for example, 202 is a common tempo. The first two equals the speed of the first movement, with the second representing the duration of the hold, and finally the third representing the speed of return to the starting position.

The following table highlights the exercises that make up the strength session in phase four of the training programme.

COURT INTERVAL GUIDELINES				
	Number of reps to aim for in the work period	Work (seconds)	Recovery (seconds)	% MWHR
Phase 1	8–12	120–180	60–90	75–80%
Phase 2	8–12	90–120	90–120	80–85%
Phase 3	12–16	60–90	90–120	85–90%
Phase 4	16–20	30–60	60–90	90% +

RUNNING INTERVAL SESSION GUIDELINES					
	Sets	Reps	Work	Recovery between reps	Recovery between sets
Phase 1	2	2	10min	1–2min	35min
Phase 2	2	4	5min	12min	35min
Phase 3	23	34	24min	30–90sec	90sec–3min
Phase 4	35	45	30–90sec	30–90sec	90sec–3min

STRENGTH SESSION IN PHASE FOUR OF THE TRAINING

Exercise	Sets	Reps	Tempo	Rest
1. One leg squat	2–3	10–15	202	60sec
2. Barbell bench press	2–3	10–15	202	60sec
3. Lateral lunge	2–3	10–15	202	60sec
4. Integrated shoulder press	2–3	10–15	202	60sec
5. Lateral pull down	2–3	10–15	202	60sec
6. Supine bridge & tuck one legged	2–3	10–15	202	60sec
7. Superman (Swiss ball)	2–3	10–15	202	60sec
8. Dynamic side bridge (each side)	2–3	60 sec	Controlled	60sec
9. One arm, one leg, front bridge	2–3	60 sec	Controlled	60sec
10. Twisting crunch (Swiss ball)	2–3	10–20	Controlled	60sec
11. Saxon bend (dumb-bell)	2–3	10–20	202	60sec

Core Stability Training

Core stability relates to the trunk of the body, and its ability to support the effort and forces from the arms and legs. Good core stability allows the muscles and joints to perform in their most effective positions. With good core stability an individual can generate power by maximizing the efficiency of their muscular effort. Core stability and muscle balance is fundamental to good training practice in order both to reduce the risk of injury and to ensure optimal physical performance.

Core stability training initially begins with simple exercises that can be completed during the cool-down phase, and once an individual has mastered the art of stabilizing muscles, the progressive exercises add movement and greater co-ordination. Each of the exercises involves contracting the abdominal muscles and holding for ten before repeating. The individual must pull their stomach up and in, and for the last exercise the individual holds the contraction, bringing the opposite hand and knee together to push against each other.

Three basic core strength exercises.

Three advanced core strength exercises.

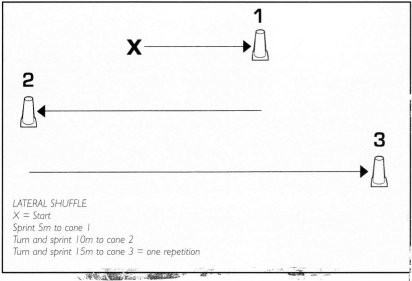

LATERAL SHUFFLE
X = Start
Sprint 5m to cone 1
Turn and sprint 10m to cone 2
Turn and sprint 15m to cone 3 = one repetition

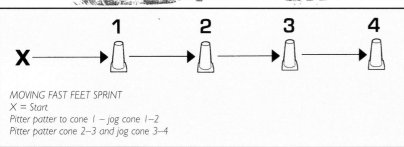

MOVING FAST FEET SPRINT
X = Start
Pitter patter to cone 1 – jog cone 1–2
Pitter patter cone 2–3 and jog cone 3–4

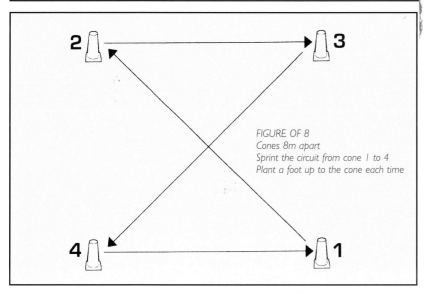

FIGURE OF 8
Cones 8m apart
Sprint the circuit from cone 1 to 4
Plant a foot up to the cone each time

Speed and agility drills.

Speed and Agility Training Programmes

Speed and agility training should be incorporated within the warm-up for the on-court sessions. This type of training develops short acceleration and agility. Within the England Netball potential training programme the individual must select three drills and repeat each one twice, allowing 90sec recovery between each.

Fitness testing, as previously discussed, will determine an individual's training level, strengths and areas for development. It is through this testing procedure that more individualized training programmes can be implemented around the key aspects of strength and conditioning. To succeed in netball requires a high level of commitment to train both on and off the court.

CHAPTER 18

NUTRITION

At international level in netball the winning margins are often narrow, and to optimize performance a player must ensure that all components of performance are attended to. In order to gain the maximum benefit from training, a player must adhere to the nutritional guidelines. Nutritionists working with élite-level athletes are able to offer sound advice on eating habits, before, during and after competition and training. Good eating habits should be promoted early, and any talented individual will receive nutritional advice and education as part of the long-term athlete development programme in netball.

In order to achieve optimal nutrition, an individual's diet must be consistent, and therefore skipping meals will impact negatively on performance. Six small to medium meals are ideal, and two to three meals are not enough. Muscles require fuel to repair, and without appropriate intake of food the muscles will feed off muscle tissue in the body, therefore leaving the body with a higher percentage of fat. Eating small and frequent meals every three hours is a positive way to controlling appetite and blood sugar levels. Protein will also be available regularly to support growth and recovery.

How Much Should I Eat?

Each day a player should strive to include food from a range of food groups in order to ensure there are correct amounts of carbohydrate, protein, vitamins and minerals in the diet. The amount of fat within the diet should be restricted to a healthy level. An individual should try and consume 60 per cent of daily energy from

carbohydrate, 25 per cent from fat and 15 per cent from protein. An individual should ensure that they try to include the recommended number of portions per food group to maintain adequate amounts of carbohydrate, protein, vitamins and minerals whilst keeping the intake of fat to a healthy level.

The Glycaemic Index of Food

Athletes in any sport should also consider the amount of carbohydrate and the glycaemic index of food. A glycaemic index relates to the speed at which food is able to raise the blood sugar levels. Thus fast carbohydrates (high glycaemic index foods) will be very useful in raising low blood sugars, and for covering brief periods of intense exercise. Slower carbohydrates (low glycaemic index foods) can be used to prevent a decrease in the blood sugar overnight, and to sustain the blood sugar during long periods of exercise. Throughout the day an individual should eat low to medium glycaemic foods, and after exercise, or as the last meal of the day, there should be an intake of high glycaemic foods.

Each individual can have a different glucose response, and a combination of foods can produce very different results between individuals. Therefore, the process

FOOD GROUP AND PORTIONS

Food group	Portions	Example of portions
Starchy foods	9–12	carbohydrate: one potato/slice of toast
Meat	3–4	75g of lean meat/50g of cheese
Fruit / vegetables	4–5	banana/1 heaped table spoon of vegetables
Dairy products	2–3	1/2 pint semi-skimmed milk/150g yoghurt
Oils and fats	2–3	1 teaspoon vegetable oil or olive oil spread

TABLE 1: GLYCAEMIC INDEX SCORES AND EXAMPLE OF FOODS

Food type	High	Medium	Low
Sugars	Honey and glucose	Table sugar	Fructose
Breads	White and bagel	Pitta bread and rye	Pumpernickel
Cereals	Weetabix	All Bran	–
Beans	Kidney	Baked and butter	Chick peas
Vegetables	Carrots	Mushrooms	Broccoli
Fruit	Watermelon	Banana	Apple
Beverages	Sports drinks	Orange juice	Milk
Snacks	Crackers	Sponge cake	Peanuts
Pasta	Pasta cooked for a longer time	Oriental noodles	Spaghetti (white)
Soups	Split pea	Onion soup	Tomato

of selecting the correct foods is highly individualized, and as a result the glycaemic index numbers should be used to provide a broad and general guideline for planning food intake before, during and after exercise.

Pre-Exercise

The pre-competition or training meal should be between 300 and 800 calories, and made up of carbohydrates with a low to medium glycaemic index score. This ensures that glucose is released into the circulation slowly, without an insulin charge. The meal should also contain small amounts of protein and fat, and should be consumed between one and two hours before the training or competition. The individual should also drink two cups (5ml/kg) of water one hour before exercise to maintain hydration levels.

AN EXAMPLE OF A PRE-EVENT MEAL

- Yoghurt, whole wheat or rye bagel and cream cheese.
- Apple slices with peanut butter, unsweetened juice.
- Six small pancakes with four tablespoons of maple syrup.

During Exercise

During training an individual should take in some form of carbohydrate during exercise of one to three hours at a high intensity. Taking in carbohydrate at half time during a game can delay fatigue between thirty and sixty minutes. Individuals will often take in carbohydrate in the form of a sports drink and this should contain 14 to 20g of carbohydrate. Individuals must not let the carbohydrate stores run out, and drinking a cup of sports drink every fifteen to thirty minutes during exercise will assist in replacing fluids, and will also replenish carbohydrate.

Post-Exercise

The replenishment of glycogen takes up to twenty hours after exercise (for example, two to three hours of continuous exercise, or fifteen to thirty minutes of high intensity exercise). An individual should ingest carbohydrate as soon after exercise as is practical; initially many athletes prefer to consume carbohydrate via a sports drink, rather than eat solid foods. When they feel ready to eat solid foods, 600g of carbohydrate should be eaten within twenty-four hours, and it is essential that they eat meals containing no less than 70 per cent carbohydrate.

AN EXAMPLE OF A POST-EXERCISE MEAL

- Consume a meal within one hour after exercise: 180–200g of moderate to high glycaemic index carbohydrates, 30–40g of protein and 20–30g of fat.
- Consume another meal three to four hours post-exercise. If the exercise is late in the evening, then breakfast should provide this next meal.
- The other meals to follow should be of low to moderate glycaemic index foods. The ratio for carbohydrate: protein:fat should be 4:3:3 for these meals.

Protein

Lean protein sources are required for muscle growth and maintenance, for the production of healthy blood cells and to strengthen immunity. The body must

---

EXAMPLES OF LEAN PROTEIN SOURCES

Food	Serving	Protein
Chicken (skinless)	110g	35g
Egg (whole)	1 large	6g
Pork (lean)	110g	35g
Tuna (water packed)	165g	40g

---

consume sufficient carbohydrate for energy purposes to ensure the protein is used to build muscle. An élite netball player requires 0.8–0.9g of protein per pound of bodyweight. Protein intake will vary according to the activity performed, the intensity and duration of the event, and the number of calories consumed.

Vitamins and Minerals

Vitamins and minerals are also an essential part of the diet, and an individual should aim to include four or five portions of fruit and vegetables per day, include plenty of low fat dairy products to boost calcium intake, and use rest days as food days where extra time is available to eat healthy foods.

The following information gives some examples of foods and the vitamins contained within them:

Vitamin A	Liver, eggs, carrots and green leafy vegetables
Vitamin B1	Meat, nuts and whole grains
Vitamin B6	Meat, fish, green leafy vegetables, whole grains
Vitamin B2	Liver, dairy produce, meat and cereal
Vitamin B12	Meat, fish and dairy produce
Vitamin C	Fruit, potatoes and white bread
Vitamin D	Dairy produce
Vitamin E	Vegetable oils, liver and green leafy vegetables
Vitamin K	Liver and green leafy vegetables

Minerals are also a vital component of an athlete's diet, and some example food sources and the minerals within them are given here:

Sodium	Salt, cheese, fish and bacon
Potassium	Vegetables, cereals and nuts
Calcium	Milk, cheese and nuts
Iron	Nuts, seeds, red meat and eggs
Zinc	Seafood and green vegetables

Calcium is a vital mineral for an athlete, and a female aged between eleven and eighteen should consume 800mg of calcium per day to promote a healthy bone structure.

Hydration

Dehydration can also contribute to fatigue and poor performance. When competing or training the body temperature rises, and in order to dispel the excess heat and prevent overheating, the body produces sweat. As the sweat evaporates from the skin, an individual will experience heat loss and body fluid loss. It is a common assumption that there can be losses of more than 2000ml of fluid during a two-hour training session. It is vital that the individual replaces all fluids lost as a result of intense netball activity. Small losses in body fluid can result in a significant reduction in physical performance, and also affect concentration, co-ordination, decision making and reaction times. It is often stated that a 3 per cent dehydration of muscle can cause a 10 per cent loss of strength and an 8 per cent loss of speed in the muscle.

A player must drink plenty of water before, during and following intense periods of exercise. The thirst mechanism is an indication that the body is already dehydrated, and so individuals must follow the good practice guidelines for maintaining a good hydration.

Each individual must ensure that the appropriate foods are combined in the diet to allow for the body to obtain energy and the forty nutrients that the body requires from foods. Therefore, an individual must eat foods from all the major food groups: for example, starchy foods (breads and potatoes), fruit and vegetables, meat and fish, milk and dairy products and fats, oils and sugary foods. Nutrition is not for consideration solely on competition days, and an individual must ensure that they have a suitable training diet.

CHAPTER 19

SPORT PSYCHOLOGY

Possessing a high level of skill and physical fitness does not necessarily guarantee success in any sport, and experienced players readily accept the importance of possessing a sound mental approach. Several psychological techniques can support a player in terms of enhancing their confidence, control, commitment and concentration. In netball the skills of goal-setting, imagery, thought-stopping and pre-performance routines are frequently used to support the performer in their training and competition.

Goal-Setting

Any player training at a high level must plan and manage their time effectively, and setting goals will help a player work towards achieving their ambitions in netball. Goal-setting encourages an individual to focus and direct their efforts on achieving personal targets and overall will enhance an individual's commitment to training and performance.

KEY POINTS

Specific: You must be precise in stating the goals.

Measurable: Performance must be measured.

Adjustable: Goals should be reviewed regularly and adjusted if necessary.

Realistic: Set goals beyond your present ability but within reach.

Time-based: For motivation, state a point in time for the goal to be achieved.

Evaluated: Review goals regularly and reflect upon progress.

Reported: Write down the goal and show this to someone else.

Effective goal setting is achieved through applying the key principles, and the acronym SMARTER is useful for any individual or coach to remember the key principles.

A coach will often work with the individual and set a range of goals, which could be either outcome, process or performance goals. Outcome goals are concerned with the end result and, although motivating, can often depend on external control factors, such as the opposition. Being outcome-focused does not always bring about a good performance as an individual becomes pre-occupied with the end result. Outcome goals are often set as long-term goals.

Performance goals are controlled fully by the performer and they often represent personal targets and standards that you want to achieve. For example, convert 85 per cent of shots taken during a match or pass with a 90 per cent accuracy rate in the match. Performance goals are often effective in the medium term and provide a stepping stone for achieving the outcome goals.

Process goals relate to the detail in terms of achieving the performance and outcome goals; for example, carry out my pre-shot routine for all shots taken at goal or release the ball from a high position. These goals ensure the individual is able to focus on specific actions, rather than being overly concerned with the outcome itself. These goals are effective in the short term, and can enhance concentration and allow the individual to focus on task-relevant thinking.

All three types of goals are important, but it is the performance and process goals that provide the foundations and step-by-step guidance for achieving the long-term ambitions.

Enhancing Concentration

Any performer must focus their attention on the relevant cues within a competitive situation, ensuring that they block out any potential distractions that could inhibit their performance. A variety of strategies can help improve concentration, and these must be learned and practised.

Distractions can come from within the individual, such as thinking about a previous error made or anger at an umpire's decision. The external distractions are from the immediate environment and include crowd or team-mate comments, and the behaviour and tactics of the opposition. There are a number of techniques that will assist a player in coping with these distractions, which are known as Concentration Cue Performance Routines, Error Parking and Imagery.

Concentration Cue Performance Routines

These cues act as triggers and ensure that a performer is able to keep their mind on the task and the present. The concentration cues can be verbal, visual or physical. A verbal cue is where a word or phrase is repeated silently at an appropriate time, for example 'ready' or 'switch on'. A visual cue involves paying attention to something specific in the environment, for example looking at a sticker on the back of the hand. Physical cues could involve taking deep breaths, bouncing on your toes or closing your eyes momentarily.

Error Parking

This is a useful technique following an error that may have occurred and here the individual creates an image in the mind to remove the distraction. For example, performers often create an image of screwing up a piece of paper and putting it into the bin.

Imagery

This is where an individual creates an experience in the mind, such as imagining yourself shooting the ball accurately or competing in a certain situation. The individual must create in their mind the information detected by the sense organs such as sounds, feelings of movement and reliving emotions. Imagery can be used in two ways: for developing confidence, controlling anxiety and improving concentration; or to strengthen and correct the performance of skilled actions.

Imagery is effective if the image is vivid and incorporates each of your senses. You must be able to influence the content of the image; for example, when shooting the ball the image must be for the duration of the three seconds allowed in the game.

Individuals will prefer to view the image either from the internal perspective (through your own eyes) or from the external perspective (as if you were seeing yourself on television). The former is useful for the mental practice of physical skills, and the latter for tactical rehearsal or when reviewing your own performance.

WHEN TO USE IMAGERY

- To improve self-confidence.
- To practise a move.
- As part of a pre-shot routine.
- During injury.
- To control anxiety and arousal.

Imagery requires practice and each individual will often have a preference for a particular sensory organ. For example, some individuals prefer to visualize shooting the ball when another would prefer to focus on the sound or the 'swish' noise of the successful shot going through the net.

Coping with Pressure

Often pressure can cause anxiety for a performer, which can ultimately impact upon an individual's ability to concentrate within a game. Arousal is a term used to describe the physiological and psychological responses of the body. Arousal can be seen on a continuum ranging from the lowest arousal level when you sleep to the extreme, which is when an individual experiences fear, anger or extreme excitement. At a point on this continuum an individual would have an ideal performance state known as the zone of optimal functioning (ZOF). Some individuals need to be psyched and fired up before a performance, whereas others tend to be quieter and calm. Every performer should work out their ZOF by reviewing performance levels and their arousal levels before a match. An individual can improve their performance if they understand the relationship between how they feel on the inside and how they perform. Techniques to reduce arousal levels include thought-stopping, imagery and appraisal-changing.

Thought-stopping is where an individual becomes sensitive to negativity and removes the negative thoughts from their mind. For example, when a negative thought comes into the mind the individual should shout 'Stop' with their inner voice or imagine a 'Stop' sign appearing.

Imagery involves the performer coping with the mental anxiety before a game by sitting in a quiet room and completing some positive imagery. Here the individual recalls good performances, sees future successes and calms their nerves by imaging relaxing scenes prior to the competition.

Appraisal-changing can be used when an individual has heightened levels of mental anxiety, perhaps while worrying about the demands of the competition, their ability and the consequences of not meeting the demands. For example, an individual may say 'This is going to be a tough match'; by reappraising the individual could change this to say

'Although this match will be tough, my training programme and preparation will allow me to cope.'

The Pre-Shot Routine for Shooters

Shooters carry with them an added pressure of being responsible for scoring for their team, so they should be adequately prepared with the psychological skills to cope with the immense pressure associated with the goal attack and goal shooter positions.

A five-step strategy has been adopted for shooters in netball that involves:

1. Ready
- Get comfortable physically and attain an appropriate mental state.
- Attempt to do things in preparation that are associated with previous best performances, and be consistent.

2. Image
- Produce a mental picture of the shooting action, think positive and feel the movement.

3. Focus
- Concentrate on one relevant feature of the situation, e.g. an imaginary spot above the centre of the shooting ring.

4. Execute
- Perform the action, but do not think about the act or the outcome.

5. Evaluate
- If time permits, use feedback to learn from the action.
- Assess the performance outcome.
- Adjust any procedure next time if necessary.

For all techniques to be successful the performer must learn and practise them regularly before they are applied in competition. A consistent approach to performance by using the techniques that work for you will ultimately lead to consistently good performances.

PART 5
COMPETITION

CHAPTER 20

MATCH PREPARATION

Any coach will readily admit that success in competition is a result of effective planning leading up to, and on the day of the event. A coach will encourage all individual players to develop their own competition routine, which represents a set of personalized activities; these

include travel, contingency planning, goal setting, psychological preparation, warm-up routines and evaluation. Any player and coach will begin planning for the competition well in advance of the day to ensure that they are well organized and focused.

A Competition Routine for Players

The coach should work with all individual players to support them in formulating their own individual routine for the

The England A Squad line up before a test match in London, and eagerly anticipate the start of the match.

competition. Key questions that a coach will ask the players in formulating their plan include:

- How much sleep do you need the night before the event?
- What food do you prefer to eat leading into the event?
- What routine do you have for packing your kit bag?
- How will you travel to the meeting point?
- When do you like to go over the game plan in your mind?
- How do you cope with family and friends leading up to the day?
- Do you have set individual exercises that you like to do in the warm-up?
- How do you control your anxiety?

A Competition Routine for the Coach

An effective coach will also prepare fully for the competition by assigning roles to staff, analysing the opposition, delivering appropriate training sessions prior to the competition, selecting the squad and team, goal setting, and communicating the game plan.

Roles

The majority of accredited clubs produce clear role descriptions and codes of conduct for the staff and volunteers in the club. However, each competition will have different administrative and domestic arrangements, and it is in the remit of head coach to ensure that roles are clarified for all staff attending the competition. Prior to the competition day there is a need to finalize several domestic issues; for example travel arrangements, accommodation, umpiring, scoring, and management roles whilst on the bench. The team manager will often take ownership of the domestic issues, and through liaison with the relevant staff and head coach, will draw up a competition schedule. This schedule will be printed and handed to players, parents and support staff so that the timings and meeting points are all clearly documented.

The management of the bench during the competition must be addressed, and the bench players will often be assigned a specific role and responsibility. Roles assigned to the bench players could be any of the following: for example, handing court players drinks during the quarter and half-time intervals, putting the balls into the bag after any warm-up, leading the bench players to warm up with five minutes remaining in the quarter, and also collating any match statistics based on tasks set by the coach.

Analysing the Opposition

A coach is expected to assess the strengths and weaknesses of the opposition, and to note any individual or unit, and team tactics and strategies. The coach must then apply this information into the training sessions leading up to the event, looking at methods that could be implemented to counteract the strengths and capitalize on weaknesses of the opposition.

An effective coach will assess the strategies employed and the technical strengths of each opposing player. Some of the typical questions a coach may seek to find the answer for when addressing the opposition are outlined below:

Goal keeper	Does she have good elevation?
	Can she mark a moving shooter effectively?
Goal defence	Is she a tight stage one defender?
	Does she follow a rotating shooter or zone the circle?
Wing defence	Does she commit for the interception?
	Is she beaten on a dodge or a straight sprint?
Centre	Does she front-cut a defender?
	Is she a main feeder of the shooters?
Wing attack	Does she attack the top of the circle edge?
Goal attack	Does she use different set-ups at the centre pass?
	Does she receive many centre passes?
	Does she use base-line runs to enter the circle?
Goal shooter	Does she move, or play a holding game?
	Does she offer for the ball out of the circle?

The coach must also assess the style of play adopted by the team, and an example of the questions to ask of the opposition could be:

- What styles of defence are used through the court (zone or man to man)?
- Do they use the overlap player to support attacking play?
- Do they front-cut, or rely on overhead passing?
- What defending strategies are used at the centre pass and back-line throw-in?
- Do players switch roles through the court?

Training Sessions and Selection

The pre-competition training must prepare players for the match, and the various team combinations must be practised. A coach will build up a firm understanding of the combinations that work effectively through communication patterns, player strengths and decision-making. The coach must work through the skills and tactics that need to be implemented in the forthcoming match, and in doing this must assess the strengths and weaknesses of each player in relation to the intended game plan. A coach will select the squad and start seven players, based upon their ability to implement the game plan that will counteract the strengths of the opposing players.

The coach must ensure that the players selected have the ability to make accurate decisions under pressure, and it is advantageous if they are flexible in their thoughts and actions.

The information below demonstrates how a Talent League coach has assessed an opposing goal shooter and subsequently selected a goal keeper to try and counteract the strengths of this key attacking player. The information noted below represents the findings from an assessment of the opposing goal shooter:

- A very static player who plays a holding game.
- Moves out of the circle to receive but is not fast.
- Is intimidated by the defender jumping when shooting.
- Likes to receive a bounce pass from an attacking player on the circle edge.

As a result of the above assessment the following goal keeper was selected:

- Has quick feet and is able to reposition when marking a shooter.
- Can intercept short passes to a shooter by reaching low and using a long arm span.
- Has excellent elevation and a well timed jump when marking the shot.

A developmental-level coach working with talented players will often prioritize the value of the competition, and may decide to use such an event for individual player development. In this instance the coach may decide that all players in the squad will be exposed, and highlight that it is a game of low priority in terms of outcome. This is where developing players can link with more experienced players in the squad, and also begin to experience higher intensity match play. The effective coach will communicate the intentions of the competition to ensure all players are well informed. Occasionally players join a squad at the higher level to experience the bench procedures and overall pressures encountered when a large crowd is present.

Goal Setting

The goal-setting process has been covered in more detail in Chapter 19; however, competition goals should be devised as a result of the following actions:

- Discussions with individual players in training sessions.
- Discussions with the squad in the final training session.
- Coach observations of the opposition.
- Coach observations and analysis of their own squad in previous matches.

A coach must ensure that not only outcome goals, but performance and process goals are set for any competition. By incorporating all three types of goal, each individual player is able to evaluate their performance accurately, irrespective of the result. The following goals were set by a coach leading into a Netball Talent League match:

Outcome Goal
- To win the match.

Performance Goals
- Achieve a 90 per cent success rate from the centre pass to shooting opportunity.
- Achieve an 80 per cent success rate of centre pass to goal scored.
- Gain six interceptions in the mid-court per quarter.
- Wing attack and centre to achieve an 80 per cent success rate for passing to a shooter.

Process Goals
- Release the ball from a balanced position, having assessed the options available.
- Two forward options must be available for the ball carrier.
- Effectively mark the player at the second stage of defence.

- Tight man-to-man for the first five minutes of each quarter.

To ensure good practice a coach should also set process goals for individuals: for example, if there is a squad member who constantly seeks out and delivers a diagonal pass that is intercepted, a goal could be 'To use the straight line option or the square pass to an overlapping player'.

Communicating the Game Plan

A coach must present the game plan during the squad meeting, and this is usually one hour prior to the match warm-up. The information covered in this meeting will simply reinforce the key issues covered in the training sessions, and will reinforce the tactical methods to be implemented. The coach should focus clearly on the positive aspects of previous performances, ensuring that all players emerge from the meeting confident and motivated. Using a facilitative style through questioning will encourage players to take ownership of the plan and to remain focused on the discussions. The game plan should be communicated concisely, and the use of visual aids to represent formations or defending set-ups will often support this process.

Effective routines will ensure that both players and support staff remain focused on their role. Ultimately the players should feel well supported, organized, and fully focused on the competition itself. Due to the effective planning, organization and presence of systematic preparation by the coach, all players should feel confident of a positive competition outcome.

CHAPTER 21

MATCH ANALYSIS

The game of netball can be analysed from a variety of perspectives, and the statistics obtained will provide the coach with immediate and accurate feedback as to individual, unit, opposition and own team performances. The focus of the observations and data gathering is determined by the game plan formulated for the team, along with the unit and individual goals set for the match. Often a statistical analysis is administered, which incorporates the use of paper and pencil techniques and a simple notation system. Statistical analysis is used, which represents a process of collecting, classifying and ultimately interpreting number-based information.

In netball there is an abundance of information that can be recorded, and the coach must limit the analysis to ensure that the findings are accurate and relate only to the aspects of primary concern.

The coach must have a clear rationale for selecting the statistical information to be gathered. Following a previous encounter with a team, the following

SHOT ANALYSIS

Symbol	Inner	Outer	Total %
✓ Score			
X Miss			
R Rebound			
E Rebound Error			
G Gain			
L Loss			

A shot analysis recording sheet.

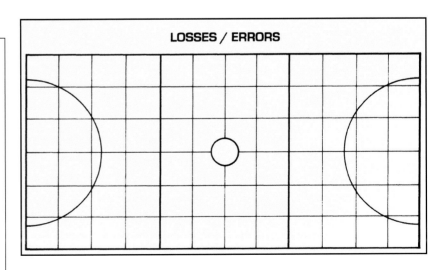

Losses and errors recording sheet.

TYPES OF ANALYSIS

- Shooting (number of attempts, success rate and location).
- Turnovers (forcing of an error or an interception gained).
- Conversions (goal scored after a turnover).
- Errors and losses of possession (player error and location).
- Patterns of play (from set plays and dead ball situations).
- Feeding the shooting circle (by whom, to whom, location and success rate).
- Patterns of play (frequency and preferences of your own and the opposing team).

information was recorded by a coach, based upon observations of her own team's performance:

- The centre pass broke down frequently and the second phase of the centre pass did not reach the edge of the circle.
- The goal attack was overused.
- The shooter relied on taking the overhead pass when in the shooting circle.

- The goal attack was feeding the ball from the circle edge to the goal shooter.
- Interceptions were gained by the opposition in the shooting circle.
- Loss of possession was recorded in the attacking third.

Following this analysis the coach was keen to record information based upon the breakdown in play noted above. As a result, the following game statistics were recorded:

- Centre pass sequence (own team).
- Success of circle feeds (own team).
- Interceptions gained by the opposition.

The above example indicates the rationale used by a coach to identify aspects of play to be recorded in a forthcoming match. The statistical analysis will provide feedback related to aspects of play that had previously broken down.

The interval is a time to reassess the game plan, and a coach will offer support and advice to players.

Using Notation

Often a notation system will utilize numbers, symbols and letters to allow for event information to be recorded at speed. The illustrations below are examples of notation systems frequently used in netball.

Netball is a game played at the higher level over four quarters, and in most school and club competitions there would be a half-time period. These intervals in a game allow the coach to feed back immediately any detail to the players by outlining what is working well, and also what corrections and adaptations need to be made to counteract the opposition. The statistical information obtained will also support a coach's decision to

substitute a player if they are unable to execute the game plan. For example, the goal attack may have missed the last five attempts at goal, indicating that she has been the weak link in the attacking unit, and the coach may decide to use a substitute.

Feedback to Players

The quarter-time intervals are for a period of 3min, and half time is 5min or 10min. Because these periods are limited, a coach must have an organized bench, and they must ensure that there is a strategy for providing feedback during the intervals. The assistant coach will often complete the notational analysis and

present this information to the coach a short time before the end of the quarter.

During the intervals of a match the court players are given seats in position order so they are sat in their specific units to receive information and feedback from the coach. A coach will often give positive feedback to the whole team, indicating what is working well overall, followed by a key aspect that needs to be addressed by the team as a whole. They will then move into the units and offer feedback on the tactics being employed, and will also identify any aspects that may need to be changed. They will then offer any individual feedback if necessary to ensure the player continues the good work, or so they can make necessary improvements in their performance.

Recording the centre pass sequence.

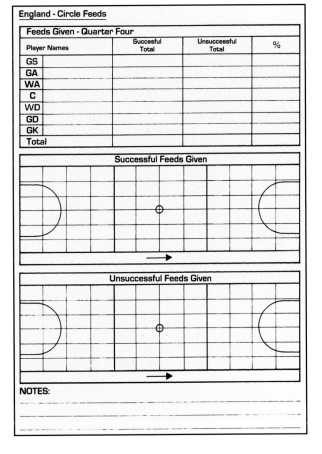

Recording the circle feeds.

Feeding into the circle can be measured using notation systems.

During the half-time period a coach will often allow players the opportunity to discuss and clarify issues between them. Often they will allow a period of time where players can hydrate and briefly reflect prior to information being presented. Any player being substituted will receive a brief explanation as to the rationale for this change, which can then be discussed in more detail in the post-match phase.

After a match it is common practice to carry out what is called a 'hot debrief', and this immediately follows the cool-down phase. Here a coach will offer feedback on the performance, and use a questioning style to encourage players to reflect on the match and note the aspects of the game plan that worked well, and also to identify aspects requiring further attention in subsequent training sessions.

A coach will also analyse this information post match to inform the content of future training sessions. They may complete the analysis to note that a player was unable to execute the game plan due to a breakdown in a specific technical skill. The accuracy of the analysis is critical to highlight the main cause of a specific breakdown in play.

The use of video recording allows the coach and players the opportunity to observe the match and specific events in subsequent training sessions. Often the result of a competition may distort a coach's evaluation, and so the playback mechanism can reinforce actions and events in more detail. For this to be effective the coach must clearly identify the focus of the observations prior to meeting the players.

Modern technology and software packages allow a coach to categorize and code the specific aspects of play: for example, the playback process will show all successful centre passes that resulted in a goal being scored, shown one after the other.

GLOSSARY

This is a glossary of words and terms used in this book and in netball. You may or may not find these words in an English dictionary, and if you do, their definitions will probably be radically different from the ones given here.

Advantage A term used by the umpire to signal that an infringement has occurred, but play does not stop. The team in possession continues to play.

Attacking team The team in possession of the ball.

Attacking third The goal third, where a team attacks the shooting circle being defended by the opposition.

Attacking unit This unit is a group of players, namely the goal shooter, goal attack, wing attack and centre, who will often set tactical strategies as a group.

Back pass When a centre player distributes the ball at the centre pass to a player behind her, which could be the goal defence or the wing defence.

Back space The area available behind the receiver to move into and receive a pass.

Ball carrier The player in possession of the ball.

Ball side The position of a player is nearer to the ball than their opponent.

Baseline run This is where a goal shooter or goal attack will enter the circle, running parallel to the goal line.

Bat When a player touches the ball with their hand in an uncontrolled manner.

Bench The place where the coach, substitutes and other support staff would sit during a game.

Bib Worn to identify the playing position of each individual.

Carioca step A cross-over action similar to a side step, where the individual will cross one foot in front of the other and then the next step would be behind the lead leg.

Centre circle The circle in the mid-third where the centre must stand to take the centre pass.

Centre pass Taken to start and also to restart the game after a goal has been scored.

Centre third The middle third on the netball court.

Circle rotation Involves the goal shooter and goal attack in the shooting circle, who move to retain the balance of the circle in terms of their positioning, both widthways and lengthways.

Channels Often used by a coach to describe the imaginary divisions of the court lengthways. The left, mid- and right channels are terms used to ensure that a player is aware of the space and width available on attack.

Circle edge The area surrounding the shooting circle, where the wing attack and centre should aim to position in order to support and pass to the shooters.

Clearing run A player may execute a clearing run to leave space or create a space for a team mate to move into.

Code of conduct An outline of guidelines for good practice and behaviour.

Contact Netball is a non-contact sport, and this means that opposing players must not physically contact each other.

Conversion After possession is gained from the opposing team, a goal is scored.

Core stability This is the ability of the trunk to support the movement of the arms and legs. With good core stability (strength in the abdominal and lower back muscles), an individual will perform safe and balanced movements, generating power and maximizing the efficiency of their muscular effort.

Court interval training Runs of various lengths and directions completed on the court to simulate the distances and directions used in a game.

Cues External factors that are visible and contribute to the decisions made.

Dead ball situation Situation where the ball has gone out of play or where an infringement has occurred on the court, and play is to restart from a set position.

Defending team The team not in possession of the ball.

Defending unit A group of players, namely the goal keeper, goal defence, wing defence and centre, who will often set tactical strategies as a group.

Double lead Moving to receive the ball, and then repositioning often by changing direction, to be an option for the same or the next pass.

Double play A player passes the ball to the receiver, and then takes the next pass.

Dynamic mobility A series of progressive muscular stretches, that incorporate movement, and relate to the movements a player will experience in the game of netball.

Execution phase A skill is divided into three phases, and the execution phase follows the preparation phase and is the point at which the action commences. The recovery, or follow through, represents the final phase after the action has occurred.

Fake or feint pass A player carries out the preparation to throw to deceive and commit the opposition.

Falling start This is when an individual will transfer their bodyweight into the direction of movement from a static position.

Fartlek A type of training often called 'speed play', which will use a variety of running speeds in a training practice.

Feeder The player repeatedly passing the ball to another player.

Field-based testing A fitness test that is not carried out in a laboratory is often netball specific and completed on the court itself.

First phase of the centre pass The first pass delivered by the centre player.

Front cut A player on attack will move in front of their opponent to receive the ball.

Front player The player nearer to the ball.

Front position A player adopts a position on the front of their opponent and is nearer to the ball.

Front space The area available in front of the individual moving to receive a pass.

Full court system Represents the set-up of players and options available for the passage of the ball through the court to the shooting circle.

Getting free The ability of a player to outwit their opponent to receive the ball.

Goal line There are two goal lines, and they are situated behind the shooting circle.

Goal third There are two of these, namely the thirds at each end of the court containing a shooting circle.

High ball A pass with a high trajectory.

Hypertrophy Where tolerance is increased to resistance exercise, and muscle mass is increased.

Infringement Where a rule is broken by a player or team, and they are subsequently penalized for it by the umpire.

Initiator The player who will make the first move, often the player nearer to the ball.

Interception Gaining possession by cutting off a pass between two opposing players.

Landing foot The first foot to contact the ground when in possession of the ball. If the player lands on both simultaneously it can then be either.

Lead Movement to receive a pass.

Lunging One leg is kept stationary, and the other takes a long stride to receive the ball.

Man-to-man Marking a player tightly, sometimes referred to as 'I v I'.

Marking Pressurizing and staying close to an opposing player, often trying to prevent them from receiving the ball or moving into a desired area of the court.

Mastery climate An environment created by the coach, which will be task focused, and the individual will measure their achievements against their own previous performances.

Mid-court area The centre-third area of the court.

Netball Super League This is the top domestic competition in England, and it is from this that the Open National Squad would be selected.

Netball Talent League A top domestic age group competition for Under 19 talented players.

Obstruction When a player defends from the incorrect distance; can also occur when a player covers the path of an opposing player by using outstretched arms.

Offer The first attacking move to receive, often called a lead.

Offside Called by the umpire when a player enters into a playing area they are not allowed to move into.

Off the ball An action by a player or players that occurs when they are not in possession of the ball, or the immediate person to receive a pass.

Options The number of players in a suitable position to receive the ball.

Overlapping player A player who moves from behind play to position at the side or ahead of the ball carrier to receive the ball.

Patterns of play The movement of players, and the pathway taken of the ball through the court to goal.

Perceptual factors The external factors that need to be considered when executing a skill.

Peripheral vision The width and depth that a player is able to see.

Pivot When an individual keeps their landing foot planted on the ground and moves to face another direction using the non-landing foot.

Preliminary move A move often used to clear space before the attacking move to receive is executed.

Protecting a space A player may mark a player and keep them away from the space they want to receive the ball in.

Quarter A netball match is played over four 15min periods, each known as a 'quarter'.

Regrounded This relates to the landing foot, which can be lifted off the ground but not placed down again whilst in possession.

Rebound An individual gains possession after an unsuccessful attempt at goal.

Re-offer Another move to receive the ball if your lead or first offer is not successful or used.

Repositioning Movement to find another space or position on the court, or to be in the best position in relation to an opponent.

Run-off The area beyond the lines of the court.

Screen Where a player protects a space for a fellow team mate to move into.

Session plan proforma The outline in a tabular format used by a coach to note down the content and organization of a coaching session.

Set play Often when the game is to restart at a centre pass or throw-in, and relates to the intended movements of players and the pathway intended for the ball.

Set-up The position of players; often relates to their starting position at a throw-in or centre pass.

Shooter One of the two players that can score a goal and go into the shooting circle (goal shooter and goal attack).

Shuffling Small side-steps in various directions, used to reposition, often when defending a player.

Square pass The ball carrier delivers the ball to a player at their side.

Stack Describes the set-up of two players, often the goal attack and wing attack at the centre pass who position one in front of the other on the third line.

Straight-line pass The ball carrier distributes a pass to a player directly on a straight line in front of them.

Switching Where two players may remain in the same position, but change roles temporarily: for example, the centre position and wing attack might do this when the ball is in the centre third. The wing attack moves ahead of the centre and does more work in the mid-court area, allowing the centre to drop into the goal third.

Take-off The first step taken when moving from a stationary position.

Taper Where the training intensity and volume will be lowered, often leading up to a major competition.

Thirds The court is divided into three thirds.

Throw-in When the ball lands on the ground outside the court, a throw-in is taken to bring the ball back into play.

Timing gate Equipment used in fitness monitoring to time individuals on sprints and agility tests. A timing gate is placed at the start and end of the sprint, and the time taken by the individual can be recorded.

Tip When a player touches the ball in an uncontrolled manner with the fingertips.

Toss-up When two players have committed an infringement simultaneously the umpire will give a toss-up, where both players face each other and their own goal. The umpire releases the ball between both players and blows the whistle at the point of releasing the ball. Both players attempt to regain possession.

Tracking Following an opponent's movements, or following the movement of the ball when defending.

Training to competition ratios The number of training sessions in relation to the number of competitions within a certain time period.

Turnover When the defending team gains possession from the attacking team.

UKCC Level Descriptors A brief outline of what the coach should be able to do at each level.

Umpire Two umpires officiate and control the game.

Windows of trainability Linked to athlete development phases, and identifies a suitable period where training will be most beneficial to an 'individual'.

USEFUL CONTACTS AND ADDRESSES

International Federation of Netball Associations
IFNA Secretariat
40 Princess Street
Manchester
M1 6DE
England

Email: ifna@netball.org
Tel: 0161 234 0025
Fax: 0161 234 0026

England Netball
Netball House
9 Paynes Park
Hitchin
Hertfordshire
SG5 1EH

Tel: 01462 442344

Netball Scotland
Suite 196
Central Chambers
93 Hope Street
Glasgow
G2 7NQ

Tel: 0141 572 0052

Welsh Netball
33–35 Cathedral Road
Cardiff
CF11 9HB

Tel: 02920 237048

Netball Northern Ireland
House of Sport
Upper Malone Road
Belfast
BT9 5LA

Tel: 02890 383806

Netball Australia
AFL House
140 Harbour Esplanade
Melbourne
VIC 3008
Australia

Email: infonet@netball.asn.au

Barbados Netball Association
PO Box 331 C
Bridgetown
Barbados
West Indies

Email: bdosna75@hotmail.com

Bermuda Netball Association
PO Box HM 1416
Hamilton
HM FX
Bermuda

Email:
Debra.Saltus@scottishre.com

Botswana National Sports Council
Unit 2
Plot 1864
Gaborone
Botswana
Africa

Email: bona@it.bw

Canadian Amateur Netball Association
44 Oakwood Avenue
Toronto
ON M6J 2V6
Canada

Email:
georgebarreiro@sympatico.ca

Cayman Islands Netball Association
PO Box 1915
Grand Cayman
Cayman Islands

Email:
lucilleseymour@yahoo.com

Cook Islands Netball Association
PO Box 208
BCI House
Level Three
Avarua
Rarotonga
Cook Islands

Email: Ngarangi.Tuavera-Pittman@portcullis-trustnet.com

Netball Fiji
PO Box 235
Suva
Fiji

Email:
patricia.rokouai@exxonmobil.com

Gibraltar Netball Association
PO Box 838
Gibraltar

Email:
djvazquez@gibtelecom.net

Grenada Netball Association
PO Box 509
St George's
Grenada

Email: jacko3gd@yahoo.com

Hong Kong Netball Association
Rm 1016 Olympic House
1 Stadium Path
So Kon Po
Causeway Bay
Hong Kong

Email: hkna@hkolympic.org

Netball Federation of India
1/1606, Mansarovar Park
Shahdara
New Delhi 110-032
India

Netball Ireland
1 Fairgreen
Saggart
Co. Dublin
Republic of Ireland

Email:
netballireland@yahoo.com
or binoda@yahoo.com

Jamaica Netball Association
Suite 9
National Arena
Kingston 6
Jamaica

Email:
jamnetball@cwjamaica.com

Netball Association of Malawi
PO Box 5209
Limbe
Malawi

Email: helene@africa-online.net

Malaysian Netball Association
Tingkat 1
Wisma OCM
Jalan Hang
Jebat 50150
Kuala Lumpur
Malaysia

Email: bolajaring_malaysia@yahoo.com

Maldives Netball Association
c/o Ministry of Youth and Sports
National Stadium
G Banafusaa
20–40

Malta Netball Association
PO Box 118
Marsa, GPO 01
Malta

Email: maltanetball@hotmail.com

Netball New Zealand
PO Box 99710
Newmarket
Auckland 1001
New Zealand

Email: mariew@netballnz.co.nz

Pakistan Federation of Netball
PO Box 3755
1.1 Chundhrighar Road
Karachi 74200
Pakistan

Email: netball@khi.paknet.com.pk

Papua New Guinea Netball Association
PO Box 5053
Boroko
National Capital District
Papua New Guinea

Email: lahuib@upng.ac.pg

Samoa Netball Association
PO Box 1887
Apia
Western Samoa

Email: president@samoanetball.ws
or maldivesnetball@avasmail.com.mv

Netball Singapore
6 Stadium Boulevard
Singapore 397797

Email: cyrus.medora@netball.org.sg

Netball South Africa
PO Box 12474
Hatfield
Pretoria 0028
South Africa

Email: portiadimu@hotmail.com

Netball Federation of Sri Lanka
26 Nandimithra Place
Balapokuna Road
Colombo 6
Sri Lanka

Email: priyangi@eureka.lk

St Kitts/Nevis Netball Association
PO Box 32
Basseterre
St Kitts
West Indies

Email: grell_hull@hotmail.com

St Lucia Netball Association
PO Box GM 898
Castries
St Lucia
West Indies

Email: liotac@hotmail.com

St Vincent and the Grenadines Netball Association
PO Box 419
St Vincent
West Indies

Email: inevo@hotmail.com

Netball Swaziland
PO Box 5546
Mbabne
Swaziland

Email: nnas@realnet.co.sz

Amateur Netball Association of Thailand
2088 Sports Authority of Thailand
Rajamangala National Stadium E220
Hua-Mark
Bangkok 10204
Thailand

Email: panwira@swu.ac.th

Trinidad and Tobago Netball Association
52 Gloster Lodge Road
Gonzales
Belmont
Trinidad
West Indies

Email: tntnetball@yahoo.com

USANA
PO Box 1105
NY 10274-1105
United States of America

Email: netballusa@aol.com

Vanuatu Netball Association
PO Box 682
Vila
Vanuatu
South Pacific

Email: eileennaganga@vanuatu.com.vu

INDEX